Legends and Lessons

Alex Telman

Published by Alex Telman, 2024.

LEGENDS AND LESSONS

First edition. October 30, 2024.

ISBN: 979-8230935544

Written by Alex Telman.

Table of Contents

Author's Note

Dear Reader,

I am thrilled to share this collection of poetry and accompanying life lessons with you. My journey into the world of mythology began as a quest for understanding—the desire to uncover the timeless truths that lie hidden within these ancient tales. Each myth and legend resonates with the fundamental questions of existence, exploring the nature of humanity, the struggles we face, and the wisdom we can glean from our collective past.

This book represents a labor of love, blending original poetry with insights that reveal the life lessons embedded in each story. Poetry has a unique power to capture the emotional essence of these narratives, allowing us to feel their weight and beauty. It is my hope that through these verses, you will not only appreciate the artistry of language but also connect deeply with the themes and lessons that are as relevant today as they were in the time of the ancients.

In crafting this anthology, I aimed to honor the rich tapestry of cultures from which these myths emerge. From Greek and Norse legends to Native American and African folklore, each tale carries its own unique perspective on life's complexities. These stories have been passed down through generations, evolving yet remaining rooted in the values and beliefs of their societies. I invite you to immerse yourself in these diverse narratives, reflecting on the cultural significance they hold and the wisdom they impart.

The life lessons explored in this book are not merely theoretical; they are practical guides for navigating our own journeys. As you read, consider how these age-old stories echo in your own experiences. Whether it's the ambition and hubris of Icarus, the resilience of Persephone, or the wisdom of the Trickster Raven, each tale challenges us to reflect on our choices and the values we hold dear.

In a world that often feels chaotic and uncertain, myths provide us with a sense of continuity and connection. They remind us that we are part of a larger narrative—one that transcends time and space. By engaging with these stories, we tap into a shared human experience that fosters empathy, understanding, and a sense of belonging.

Thank you for joining me on this journey through the realms of myth and legend. May these stories inspire you to embrace the lessons they offer, encouraging you to explore the depths of your own humanity and the beauty of the world around you. Let us continue to learn from the past as we forge our paths into the future, drawing strength from the wisdom of those who came before us.

Yours sincerely,

- *Alex Telman*

Ps: Hat tip Lucas Andrade and Pexels for the book cover

Introduction

In the vast tapestry of human history, myths and legends have served as the threads that weave together our shared experiences, aspirations, and fears. They offer glimpses into the very essence of what it means to be human—our struggles, triumphs, and the age-old questions that haunt our existence. This collection, "Legends and Lessons: 36 Myths Unveiled," invites you to embark on a journey through the realms of the extraordinary, where gods and mortals intertwine, and the line between reality and fantasy blurs.

What sets this book apart is its unique structure: each myth is accompanied by an original poem that captures its spirit, alongside an exploration of the life lessons embedded within the tale. Through poetry, we delve into the emotional core of these narratives, while the accompanying explanations illuminate the profound insights that can be drawn from each story. This dual approach enriches the reading experience, offering both artistic interpretation and practical wisdom.

Every myth carries with it a seed of truth, a lesson waiting to unfurl. From the fire brought to humanity by Prometheus to the eternal struggle of Sisyphus, these stories explore the intricacies of human nature, the consequences of our choices, and the universal themes that connect us all. Each tale serves as a mirror, reflecting our own lives and the moral quandaries we face. Through the lens of mythology, we confront our fears, embrace our ambitions, and ponder our place in the cosmos.

Consider the poignant tale of Orpheus and Eurydice, a narrative steeped in love, loss, and the lengths we will go to for those we cherish. Orpheus, a gifted musician, descends into the underworld, defying the natural order in a desperate bid to reclaim his beloved. This heart-wrenching journey is not merely a story of love; it is a profound exploration of the human condition—of grief, hope, and the ultimate acceptance of loss. Through Orpheus's tale, we learn that while love may drive us to great heights, it can also lead us to profound sorrow.

The stories in this anthology are as varied as the cultures from which they originate. From the fierce warriors of Norse mythology, who grapple with destiny and honor, to the wise tricksters of African folklore who challenge the status quo, each legend offers a unique perspective on life's complexities. In "The Tale of the Baba Yaga," we are introduced to a fearsome witch whose enigmatic nature serves as a reminder of the unknown forces that govern our lives. The walking house on chicken legs symbolizes the unpredictability of existence, teaching us that embracing fear can lead to self-discovery and empowerment.

Throughout history, myths have served not only as entertainment but also as vital cultural touchstones. They provide a framework for understanding the world and our place within it. The lessons imparted by these tales are timeless, resonating through the ages, offering guidance in an ever-changing world. As we delve into the legends of ancient civilizations—the Greeks, Romans, Egyptians, and beyond—we uncover the foundational beliefs that shaped societies and influenced generations.

Consider the allegorical journey of Jason and the Argonauts as they pursue the Golden Fleece. This tale is more than an adventurous quest; it is a deep exploration of leadership, betrayal, and the ethical dilemmas that accompany ambition. As Jason navigates the treacherous waters of loyalty and deception, readers are compelled to reflect on their own choices and the moral implications of their actions. Through the trials of Jason and his companions, we learn that the path to greatness is often fraught with obstacles, requiring not only bravery but also wisdom and integrity.

In the realm of mythology, animals often play a crucial role, embodying traits that teach us about ourselves and the world around us. The stories of dragons, whether they symbolize power, greed, or wisdom, remind us of the duality present in all beings. In "The Chinese Dragon and the Pearl," the dragon becomes a guardian of prosperity and balance, illustrating the relationship between power and responsibility. These narratives challenge us to consider how we wield our own influence and the impact it has on our communities and the environment.

Equally compelling are the tales that explore the cycle of life and death, such as that of Persephone and Hades. This poignant story of love and loss illuminates the themes of transformation and renewal, encouraging us to embrace change as an integral part of existence. The descent into the underworld signifies the inevitable challenges we face, while Persephone's eventual return heralds the promise of rebirth and the cyclical nature of life. These themes resonate deeply, reminding us that hardship often precedes growth and that endings can lead to new beginnings.

Mythology serves as a powerful vehicle for exploring the complexities of human emotion and experience. The myth of Icarus, who flew too close to the sun, illustrates the dangers of hubris and unchecked ambition. This cautionary tale warns against the perils of overreaching, reminding us that our aspirations must be tempered with humility and wisdom. In our pursuit of greatness, we must remain grounded, aware of the limits of our own capabilities.

The stories compiled in this anthology not only reflect cultural values but also explore the existential questions that define our humanity. "The Legend of Gilgamesh," for example, delves into the search for immortality and the nature of friendship, prompting us to consider what truly matters in our lives. Is it the pursuit of everlasting glory, or is it the connections we forge along the way? As Gilgamesh navigates his journey, we are reminded of the importance of relationships and the legacies we leave behind.

As you embark on this literary voyage through "Legends and Lessons: 36 Myths Unveiled," prepare to encounter not just fantastical beings and heroic exploits but also the profound lessons embedded within each narrative. The original poems will evoke the emotions tied to these ancient tales, while the accompanying explanations will guide you through the moral landscapes they present. These tales invite you to reflect on your own life's journey, to ponder the choices you make, and to consider the deeper truths that bind us as a human family.

Let these myths and legends serve as a source of inspiration, guiding you through the labyrinth of existence and illuminating the paths you choose to tread. In the end, the wisdom of these stories is not confined to the pages of history; it lives on in our hearts and minds, echoing through time as we seek to understand ourselves and the world around us. Embrace the adventure, for the journey of myth is one that leads to self-discovery and enlightenment, revealing the timeless truths that continue to shape our lives today.

“Prometheus and Fire” – The Greek Titan who defied Zeus by giving humanity the gift of fire, symbolizing rebellion and knowledge.

Prometheus, a Titan, defied Zeus by stealing fire from the gods and giving it to humanity. This act symbolized rebellion and the gift of knowledge, as it allowed humans to advance and thrive. For his defiance, Prometheus was punished by Zeus, enduring eternal torment. His story represents the struggle between divine authority and the quest for enlightenment.

I

On Olympus' heights, where night and heaven merge,

Prometheus stood, his gaze defying fate,

A Titan’s heart on heaven’s edge did surge,

To steal a gift none could replicate.

Amidst the gods’ resplendent, cold disdain,

He dared to bridge the void with mortal flame,

Unyielding will, though bound in chain and pain,

To spark within the dark a burning claim.

From realms where celestial light is bound,

He grasped the ember of eternal night,

A fire to break the cold of mortal ground,

To guide through shadows with a fervent light.

The gods, in loftiness and scornful might,

Saw their dominion fade into the night.

II

Not born of vanity, but from a cause,

He sought to lift the shroud from man's dark plight,

To end the chains of an eternal pause,

To bring forth dawn from out the starless night.

He wrested light from realms where spirits tread,

To kindle warmth in hearts, to banish chill,

A flame of knowledge where the cold had spread,

A gift transcending destiny and will.

The Titan's chains, though bound in cruel deceit,

Could not the blaze of spirit ever bind,

For from Prometheus, man's ascent did meet,

A gift of wisdom, ever unconfined.

Yet gods in anger, fierce with ancient wrath,

Would stifle fire's breath, their power to clash.

Zeus, upon his throne, with thunder's might,

Pronounced eternal torment for the theft,

An eagle's beak would tear the flesh of light,

While chains of fate would leave Prometheus left.

The heavens echoed with a mournful cry,

The Titan's flesh was torn, yet spirit soared,

A fiercer blaze within his steadfast eye,

An eternal flame that none could ever shun.

The cosmos' wrath could not his spirit bind,

Nor chains confine the fire's surging flight,

For Prometheus' gift, both wise and kind,

Had bridged the chasm 'twixt the heavens and the night.

The gods, in fear, beheld their power wane,

As man ascended from their shadowed reign.

III

Upon the rock, where ages' shadows creep,

The Titan's agony, a cruel decree,

The eagle's beak, relentless in its sweep,

Yet in Prometheus, a fire's symphony.

His flesh was torn, but within his heart did blaze,

A fiercer light, unyielding in the dark,

A cosmic flame that pierced the stygian haze,

A gift transcending time and divine mark.

The heavens trembled as the Titan's flame,

Lit the sky, and gods' dominion shook,

A force of will beyond their wrath and claim,

A fire eternal in its sacred look.

The gods, in dread, beheld the flame's ascent,

Their power waned, their thrones no longer held,

For Prometheus' gift, in wisdom spent,

A bridge from mortal to divine dispelled.

Thus, the Titan's flame endures and grows,

In every spark, a truth that ever shows.

IV

Prometheus, bound, yet with an inner blaze,

Beheld mankind, their hearts aflame with fire,

His suffering, though vast, gave birth to praise,

A gift of life, of thought, and pure desire.

The fire's warmth ignited dreams and lore,

A legacy transcending time and place,

Though Titans suffer, their gifts explore,

The realms of thought and vision, broad and grace.

The gods may rage, their power dark and grim,

Yet man, inspired, ascends beyond their might,

In Titan's gift, the world's eternal hymn,

A tale where wisdom casts its fiery light.

Thus, Prometheus' flame endures, alight,

In every spark, a truth of endless light.

LIFE LESSONS

The story of Prometheus and fire is rich with lessons that resonate across time and culture, offering valuable insights into the human experience.

First and foremost, Prometheus embodies the pursuit of knowledge. By stealing fire from the gods and giving it to humanity, he highlights the transformative power of enlightenment. Fire symbolizes not only physical warmth and light but also intellectual and creative advancement. This act serves as a reminder that knowledge is a fundamental human right, essential for progress. The story encourages us to seek understanding, challenge the status quo, and embrace curiosity, even when the journey is fraught with danger.

Courage and sacrifice are central themes in Prometheus's tale. His defiance of Zeus demonstrates the strength required to stand up against oppressive authority for the greater good. This teaches us that true bravery often involves risking personal comfort and safety to benefit others. Prometheus willingly faces the wrath of the gods, suggesting that the well-being of humanity is worth the sacrifice. In our lives, we may face similar choices where we must weigh our comfort against the needs of others, pushing us to act in ways that promote justice and compassion.

However, the story also serves as a cautionary tale about the consequences of rebellion. Prometheus endures severe punishment for his actions, which emphasizes that defiance can lead to significant repercussions. This lesson urges us to consider the potential fallout of our choices, reminding us that while standing up for what is right is noble, it can also lead to personal suffering.

Moreover, fire's dual nature symbolizes the complexity of progress. While it brings warmth, safety, and innovation, it can also lead to destruction. This aspect of the story warns us to approach knowledge and technology with responsibility. We must recognize that our advancements can have both positive and negative impacts, urging us to use our creativity wisely.

Ultimately, the tale of Prometheus encourages us to harness our ingenuity and resilience. It reminds us that we hold the power to shape our destinies through knowledge and courage, highlighting the importance of balancing ambition with responsibility.

"Orpheus and Eurydice" – A tragic Greek love story of a musician who tries to rescue his wife from the underworld.

Orpheus, a gifted musician, descends into the Underworld to retrieve his wife, Eurydice, who died tragically. Using his enchanting music to soften the gods' hearts, he is granted permission to lead her back to the living world on the condition he must not look back at her until they are both in the light. Overcome by doubt, Orpheus turns to gaze at Eurydice just before reaching the surface, causing her to vanish forever into the shadows.

I

When twilight drapes the heavens in its shade,

And shadows weave through realms of spectral grace,

Orpheus, whose melodies serenade,

Seeks lost Eurydice through death's dark space.

A bard whose heart, ignited by love's fire,

Now wanders through the realm where sorrows creep,

His lyre, a beacon through the realms of ire,

A fragile light where spectral phantoms weep.

Eurydice, by fate's relentless hand,

Was cast into the depths of shadowed night,

Her essence lost where death's dark shadows stand,

Her beauty veiled from mortal's yearning sight.

Orpheus, with melodies that could enthrall,

Ventured where mortal souls would scarcely dare,

His song, a plea in Hades' somber hall,

To bring his love from sorrow's dark despair.

II

Through realms where shadows twist and mournful woe,

And phantoms of the past in darkness blend,

He roams where time and space in slow decay

Unravel, where the echoes never end.

The stones, once cold, now weep in mournful grace,

And spirits stir beneath his music's plea,

Till Persephone, with her gentler face,

Entreats her lord to grant his heart's decree.

Yet in the gloom where spectral whispers moan,

His love appeared, a fleeting phantom's shade,

But shadows wrapped her form in chains alone,

A vision by the spectral light betrayed.

The god of death, with eyes of frozen steel,

Declared, "Turn not your gaze, nor seek her shade,"

Yet Orpheus, defiant in his zeal,

Braved the darkness where the fates had laid.

In mournful strains and echoes fraught with dread,
His song descended through the caverned gloom,
Each note a lament for love that now lay dead,
A requiem within the shadowed tomb.
The lyre, once ablaze with love's bright light,
Now draped in sorrow's dark, oppressive shroud,
A testament to hope's diminished flight,
Its strains a murmur in the darkness loud.

III

In Hades' realm, where light and love decay,
His music faced the judgment of the cold,
A struggle where the shadows cruelly lay,
Revealed the limits of a heart so bold.
Orpheus, with lyre broken, bare in hand,
Stood solitary in the darkened sea,
For in the depths where spectral shades expand,
His love had fled beyond his plea.
A tale of passion and of fate entwined,
Yet bound by chains of destiny's cruel might,
His song, a beacon through the dark confined,
Now faded in the cavern of the night.
The lyre's strings, though touched by death's cruel breath,

Remain a symbol through the depths of pain,

A love that battled 'gainst the chains of death,

A flame extinguished, but not in vain.

IV

Thus Orpheus's lament endures in woe,

A haunting echo through the folds of time,

A symbol of a love that sought to show

Its power through the shadows' cruel chime.

The lyre's strains, though bound by death's cruel hand,

Still speak of love where mortal dreams are fraught,

A story of a heart that dared to stand,

And sought to shine in realms where hope is caught.

In silence where the night and sorrow blend,

The echoes of his lyre's mournful plea,

Reveal a love that braved the vale of fear,

And in its loss, the soul's true fire burns.

Orpheus's song, with echoes fraught and clear,

Continues where the shadows twist and turn,

A tale of love that braved the vale of fear,

And in its loss, the soul's true fire burns.

The story of Orpheus and Eurydice is a timeless Greek myth that delves deep into themes of love, loss, and the complexities of human emotions. It offers several important life lessons that resonate with audiences across generations.

First and foremost, the tale emphasizes the power of love. Orpheus, a gifted musician, is driven by his profound love for Eurydice, which compels him to descend into the underworld to retrieve her. This act highlights the lengths to which individuals will go for those they love. It serves as a reminder that love can inspire incredible courage and resilience. When faced with insurmountable odds, the strength of our emotions can propel us to undertake daunting challenges.

Another significant lesson revolves around the nature of grief. After Eurydice's untimely death, Orpheus is overwhelmed by sorrow, a universal experience that everyone can relate to. His music, which moves even the souls in the underworld, underscores the therapeutic power of artistic expression in coping with loss. This teaches us that while grief is an inherent part of life, finding ways to express and process it—through art, music, or conversation—can provide solace and healing.

The story also serves as a cautionary tale about the consequences of doubt. Orpheus is instructed not to look back at Eurydice until they have safely emerged from the underworld. However, his anxiety and uncertainty lead him to glance back, resulting in her permanent loss. This moment illustrates how doubt can undermine our intentions and aspirations. It teaches us the importance of trust—both in ourselves and in our relationships. Learning to trust can empower us to move forward without the burden of fear and regret.

Moreover, the myth highlights the fragility of life. Eurydice's sudden death serves as a stark reminder that life is unpredictable and fleeting. This aspect of the story encourages us to cherish our loved ones and express our feelings while we have the opportunity. It prompts reflection on the importance of appreciating the present moment, as the beauty of life often lies in its transience.

Finally, the tale underscores the value of acceptance. Orpheus's struggle against the finality of death highlights the inevitability of loss. Through his journey, we learn that acceptance is a crucial part of the human experience. While we may long for what has been lost, embracing the reality of our situation can lead to personal growth and resilience. It teaches us that, while grief may be profound, learning to carry the memories of those we love can ultimately enrich our lives.

In summary, the story of Orpheus and Eurydice offers a rich exploration of love, grief, trust, and acceptance. It encourages us to navigate our emotions thoughtfully, appreciate the fleeting nature of life, and recognize the strength of love in overcoming even the most daunting challenges.

"Hercules and the Nemean Task" – Focus on one of Hercules' twelve labors; slaying the Nemean lion.

Hercules, a legendary hero of Greek mythology, was tasked with twelve labors as penance. One of these was to slay the Nemean Lion, a fearsome beast with an impenetrable hide. After a fierce struggle, Hercules overcame the lion using his immense strength, ultimately skinning it to wear as a symbol of his triumph and strength. This labor exemplifies his heroic feats and the struggle between mortal determination and divine challenge.

I

On ancient hills where time's shadows play,

Where shattered pillars whisper lost array,

There prowled a lion born of primal fire,

Its wrath transcending earthly realms entire.

Nemea's vale, beneath the gods' dark snare,

Held in its grasp the beast beyond compare.

The hero, bound by fate's unyielding chain,

Ascended to confront this fierce domain.

Hercules, by destiny's command,

Entered the realm where shadows twist and strand.

This labor, steeped in mythic arcane dread,

Would test where mortal fears and fates are wed.

The vale resounded with the gods' deep lore,

Of ancient wars and cosmic darkness' roar.

Thus Hercules, with strength and purpose bright,

Tread through twilight's veil to face the night.

II

Through dusky paths where echoes softly wail,

Hercules pursued the lion's dark trail.

His gaze, like stars that pierce the veiled abyss,

Tracked the lion's breath, a primal hiss.

The lion's hide, a cloak of cosmic scorn,

Defied the blade where divine wrath was born.

Where steel fell short, the hero's will prevailed,

In strength and spirit where the gods had hailed.

The lion's roar, a chant from chaos' core,

Reverberated through the night's dark lore.

Each clash a stanza in fate's grim hymn,

Where gods and mortals meet on twilight's rim.

Hercules, with sinew taut and spirit keen,

Wrestled through shadows where the gods convene.

In cosmic dance, where myth and mortal blend,

He grappled with the lion to the end.

III

Beneath the moon's cold gaze, the struggle cried,

Where mortal might and divine wrath collide.

The lion's form, a shadow vast and deep,

Defied the hero's will with endless sweep.

Yet Hercules, with valor's sacred flare,

Gripped the beast as constellations stare.

The beast fell silent, stilled by hero's might,

Its roar now whispers in the starry night.

The hero stood amidst the silence vast,

His visage marked by triumph's solemn cast.

Yet in his eyes, a depth both stark and bright,

Reflected ancient gods and cosmic fight.

The lion's hide, a trophy draped in dusk,

Enshrouded Hercules in twilight's musk.

For in the weave of this celestial seam,

Lay echoes of a hero's timeless dream.

IV

The labor's end, the hero's quest fulfilled,

Returned from realms where gods and mortals willed.

The lion's hide, a mantle of the fray,

Draped Hercules in twilight's fading ray.

Yet in his gaze, a truth both vast and clear,

A mirrored tale where fate and man draw near.

The myth unveils, beneath the mortal guise,

A struggle where the divine and human rise.

In tales of ancient toil and spectral night,

Where hero's strength and fate's eternal light,

The labor speaks of more than mortal claim—

A truth where destiny and dreams are the same.

For Hercules, in grappling with his dread,

Found wisdom where the gods' paths are spread.

The trials faced and victories won,

Reflect the heart where human dreams are spun.

LIFE LESSONS

The story of Hercules and his twelve labors is filled with lessons about perseverance, bravery, and the complexity of human nature. One particularly notable labor is the slaying of the Nemean Lion, which serves as a powerful illustration of these themes.

The Nemean Lion was a fearsome creature, invulnerable to conventional weapons. Hercules faced a seemingly insurmountable challenge when tasked with defeating this beast. This labor teaches us about the importance of adaptability and resourcefulness. Hercules quickly realizes that traditional methods won't work against the lion's impenetrable skin. Instead, he uses his intellect and strength to outsmart the creature. By employing a different approach, he demonstrates that challenges often require innovative solutions.

This lesson reminds us to think creatively when faced with obstacles, rather than relying solely on familiar methods.

Additionally, the labor highlights the theme of courage in the face of fear. The Nemean Lion symbolizes not only a physical threat but also the fears and doubts we all encounter in our lives. Hercules, despite knowing the lion's ferocity, confronts his fears head-on. His bravery teaches us that facing our fears is a necessary part of growth. Rather than avoiding daunting situations, we should confront them directly, as this can lead to personal development and newfound strength.

Moreover, the labor emphasizes the importance of determination and hard work. Hercules does not give up after the initial confrontation with the lion fails; instead, he persists in his quest. This persistence is crucial in achieving goals, whether in mythical labors or our daily lives. The story encourages us to maintain a strong work ethic and resilience, even when the path forward seems daunting.

Finally, the slaying of the Nemean Lion serves as a reminder of the duality of strength and vulnerability. While Hercules embodies immense physical power, he also shows humility and a willingness to learn. By recognizing that brute force alone won't suffice, he demonstrates that true strength lies in understanding one's limitations and the need for strategic thinking. This nuanced view of strength encourages us to embrace both our capabilities and our vulnerabilities.

The labor of slaying the Nemean Lion imparts valuable life lessons about adaptability, courage, determination, and the multifaceted nature of strength. It reminds us that while challenges may seem formidable, a thoughtful approach and unwavering resolve can lead to triumph. By confronting our fears and embracing innovative solutions, we can navigate life's obstacles with confidence and resilience.

“Persephone’s Descent” – The Greek myth of the goddess of spring and her descent into the underworld, symbolizing the cycle of life and death.

Persephone, the goddess of spring, is kidnapped by Hades, the god of the underworld. Her absence causes the earth to fall into winter. Persephone’s mother, Demeter, grieves and neglects the earth, leading to eternal winter. Eventually, a compromise is reached: Persephone will spend part of the year with Hades and the rest on earth, thus explaining the cycle of the seasons.

I

When winter’s hand with ice entwines,

And shadows cloak the earth’s confines,

A tale of old in silence stirs,

Where frost and fate’s dark whisper blurs.

The earth, beneath in slumber's spell,

Shivers where coldest shadows dwell,

Yet spring’s own queen with flowers crowned,

Her laughter on the meadows found.

Persephone, with garlands fine,

Among the blooms, did dance and shine,

Her spirit weaving through the green,

In fields where light and life convene.

Yet from the depths where dark roots bind,

A god of shadows, cruelly blind,

Hades, in his chthonic keep,

Yearned for the soul he longed to reap.

II

From realms where roots of sorrow twist,

The king of night and mist did list,

His eyes upon the maiden's light,

To snatch her from the day and flight.

In chariot of somber grace,

He crossed the veiled and shadowed space,

To claim the spring's own radiant crown,

And drag her to his darkened town.

The earth, bereft of spring's embrace,

Felt chill descend, a mournful trace,

As Hades' grasp with shadows tight,

Consumed the warmth and stole the light.

Persephone, in bloom's demise,

Was drawn into the shadow's guise,

Her laughter stilled, her joy erased,

By darkness that her light displaced.

The blossoms turned to hues of grey,

The skies were draped in twilight's sway,

Spring's warmth was but a distant dream,

Lost in the night's engulfing scheme.

III

In realms where echoes softly freeze,

And silence hangs like autumn's leaves,

The queen of night with crown of dread,

Wore sorrow's veil upon her head.

Hades, in his spectral throne,

Ruled where shadows thickened, grown,

Yet found within his dark domain,

A love that bore a timeless strain.

Persephone, with heart afire,

Felt the weight of love's entire,

Her tears, a river cold and deep,

In shadows' clasp, her soul did weep.

In darkness where no light could pierce,

Where day's warmth could not reappear,

She bore the cost of love's cruel chain,

And faced the endless, shadowed pain.

Yet through the gloom, a glimmer bright,

Of dawn's hope in the deepest night,

A spark that kindled in the dark,

Where love's light left its eternal mark.

IV

Each year the cycle spins once more,

The earth revives with blooms restored,

Persephone ascends the sky,

To greet the earth with verdant eye.

Yet whispers from the underworld,

In winter's cold, their voices curled,

For life and death in seamless bind,

Reveal a truth both harsh and kind.

Their love, a thread through time's own weft,

Through death's embrace and spring's bequest,

Unveils a dance where light and dark,

In endless cycle leave their mark.

In realms where shadows and light blend,

Persephone and Hades' fates,

Their love, a thread that will not end,

Through time's embrace and heaven's gates.

LIFE LESSONS

The myth of Persephone and Hades is a powerful tale that explores themes of transformation, balance, and the cyclical nature of life and death. At its heart, the story illustrates several profound life lessons that resonate across cultures.

First and foremost, the myth highlights the concept of transformation through adversity. When Persephone is taken to the underworld by Hades, she undergoes a significant change. Initially a goddess of spring, her descent into darkness represents a profound personal trial. This teaches us that adversity can lead to growth and transformation. Just as Persephone emerges from the underworld with newfound wisdom, we too can find strength and resilience in our challenges, shaping our identities through our experiences.

The story also emphasizes the importance of balance between light and dark. Persephone's dual existence—as both the goddess of spring and the queen of the underworld—symbolizes the necessity of embracing both joy and sorrow in life. This balance is essential for personal growth. The seasons mirror this duality; spring represents renewal and hope, while winter signifies rest and reflection. Recognizing that both light and dark have their place in our lives can help us navigate the ups and downs with greater acceptance and understanding.

Additionally, the myth illustrates the concept of the cycle of life and death. Persephone's annual return to the surface marks the arrival of spring, signifying rebirth and renewal, while her descent to the underworld represents the inevitability of death and decay. This cycle serves as a reminder that life is a continuous ebb and flow. Embracing the inevitability of change allows us to appreciate the fleeting beauty of life, fostering a deeper appreciation for the present moment.

Moreover, the story teaches us about the significance of choice and agency. While Persephone is initially taken against her will, she ultimately claims her power and plays an active role in her destiny. This lesson encourages us to recognize our ability to make choices in our own lives, even in difficult circumstances. It reminds us that we can assert our agency and shape our paths, regardless of external influences.

Finally, the myth underscores the theme of love and connection. Persephone's relationship with Hades, while complex, illustrates how love can transcend boundaries. Their bond, though born from an abduction, evolves into a partnership that unites the realms of the living and the dead. This aspect of the story teaches us that love can emerge from unexpected situations and that connections can bring meaning to our lives, even in times of hardship.

The myth of Persephone and Hades offers rich insights into transformation, balance, the cyclical nature of existence, agency, and love. By reflecting on these lessons, we can navigate the complexities of life with greater resilience, appreciation, and understanding of our own journeys.

“Icarus and Daedalus” – The story of hubris and ambition as Icarus flies too close to the sun.

Daedalus, a master craftsman, builds wings of wax and feathers for himself and his son, Icarus, to escape imprisonment. Despite warnings, Icarus flies too close to the sun, melting the wax. He falls into the sea, and Daedalus mourns his hubris and loss.

I

In Crete’s deep labyrinth, where shadows weave,

A father shapes the heavens with his hand.

Daedalus, in silence, dares believe—

A son’s bright flight beyond the mortal strand.

Beneath the sun’s relentless, ancient glare,

Their wings extend like myths upon the sky.

The heavens call, a beacon rare and fair—

A crown of light no mortal soul can buy.

Yet Icarus, impassioned by the flame,

Seeks not the wisdom of his father’s art.

He craves the fire, dismisses all acclaim,

And burns the truth where dreams and folly start.

In shadows of the maze, their journey begins,

Their hearts in rhythm with the past's refrain.

Daedalus, with foresight in his wings,

Prepares them both for loss, for gain, for pain.

II

They climb where air and dream begin to blur,

In realms where time and myth entwine and sway.

The sun, a golden threshold, does concur—

Yet melts the wax that binds them on their way.

The sky, a vast expanse of shifting hues,

Holds promises and dangers intertwined.

With every beat, the wings begin to lose,

And in their flight, the sun's cruel grasp they find.

Ambition flickers—feathered hopes unspun,

Turned to ashes scattered on the breeze.

The father's warnings fade, like ghosts undone,

Where hubris rises over stormy seas.

Their ascent is fraught with echoes from the past,

Of tales where pride and downfall intertwine.

The air grows thin, the sun a fiery blast—

And Icarus, in dreams, begins to pine.

Daedalus, with dread, beholds the steep,

A spiral broken, lost to fleeting gleam.

The wings dissolve like shadows in their sleep,

As Icarus falls deeper in his dream.

The sea, a mirror to the heart's abyss,

Catches the silent shadow of the fall.

Where once was fire, the waves reclaim their kiss—

And dreams dissolve where echoes softly call.

The sun, a tyrant in its golden rage,

Turns hope to dust upon the winds of fate.

The waxen wings, now melting in the stage,

Are symbols of ambition's harsh debate.

Each feather lost is like a hope undone,

A dream that melts beneath the blinding glare.

And Icarus, in heat, begins to run—

His flight, now reckless, lost to burning air.

III

In sunlight's forge, the wings unweave and break—

And Icarus falls from heaven's fraying thread.

What once was hope becomes a hollow ache

Of shattered light, the sky's bright hunger fed.

His cries, once vibrant, fade into the sky,

A waning echo in the boundless blue.

The sun, indifferent, watches dreams go by,

And Icarus's fall is stark and true.

Daedalus, his heart a forge of grief,

Cries out to skies that echo with the void.

To watch his son fall back to earth beneath—

Is to unlearn the dream they both enjoyed.

A truth etched deep in air, in fire, in flight,

Where reaching high becomes the price we pay.

In touching light, we lose our clearest sight—

Yet still we strive, though knowing we betray.

The ocean's depths now cradle what remains,

A silent requiem to unbridled dreams.

The waves, in rhythm, hide the burning pains—

A final resting place for sunlit schemes.

Yet in this fall, there lies a hidden grace,

A lesson penned in the sky's vast cruel script.

That daring flight, though marred by its embrace,

Is but a step where human limits slip.

IV

Let Icarus's tale grow quiet in the wind,

A parable of fire, sky, and soul.

In striving high, we learn where truths are thinned—

To touch the heavens is to crack the whole.

For in the arc between the ground and sky,
Where dreams and limits intertwine and bend,
The truth of wings is not that we must fly—
But that the fall is not the final end.
In every rise and every swift descent,
We trace the contours of our fleeting span.
To grasp at stars and face the dark lament
Is to understand the limits of man.
For in our reach, in every failed ascent,
We find the measure of our boundless quest.
The balance sought, in spirit and in spent,
Is where our deepest truths are manifest.
In shadows cast by sun and dream alike,
Where Icarus's tale becomes our own,
We learn that light is both the path and spike,
And in the fall, our wisdom is well shown.
Thus, let the tale of wings and fire endure,
A myth to guide those who would seek the skies.
For in the striving, there's a truth so pure—
That in our fall, the heart of wisdom lies.

The story of Icarus and Daedalus is a poignant Greek myth that conveys significant life lessons about ambition, hubris, and the consequences of one's choices. At its core, the tale serves as a cautionary narrative that resonates with the human experience.

First and foremost, the myth underscores the dangers of hubris, or excessive pride. Daedalus, a master craftsman, creates wings for himself and his son Icarus, allowing them to escape from Crete. Despite his father's warnings not to fly too high or too low, Icarus is overwhelmed by the exhilaration of flight and, driven by ambition, ascends toward the sun. This act of defiance illustrates the perils of overestimating one's abilities and disregarding wise counsel. The lesson here is clear: when ambition blinds us to our limitations, we risk catastrophic consequences.

Additionally, the story highlights the importance of balance and moderation. Icarus's failure to heed his father's advice about flying at a safe altitude serves as a metaphor for the need for balance in our pursuits. Just as Icarus's reckless ascent leads to his downfall, we are reminded that extreme actions—whether in ambition, work, or personal endeavors—can lead to negative outcomes. Embracing moderation in our aspirations can help us achieve our goals without jeopardizing our well-being.

The tale also emphasizes the significance of responsibility and consequences. Daedalus, though a brilliant inventor, faces the repercussions of his creations. Icarus's tragic fate is a direct result of his choices, reflecting the idea that our actions have far-reaching effects. This serves as a reminder that we must take responsibility for our decisions, as they shape not only our lives but also the lives of those around us.

Moreover, the story illustrates the concept of self-awareness. Icarus's failure to recognize his limits ultimately leads to his demise. This lesson encourages us to cultivate self-awareness and to understand our capabilities and boundaries. By being mindful of our strengths and weaknesses, we can navigate challenges more effectively and avoid pitfalls caused by overconfidence.

Finally, the myth of Icarus and Daedalus speaks to the theme of the relationship between freedom and constraint. While the wings symbolize the desire for freedom and the pursuit of dreams, they also come with inherent risks. The story invites us to reflect on the balance between pursuing our passions and recognizing the constraints imposed by reality. True freedom involves understanding the limits of our actions and making choices that align with our values and responsibilities.

In conclusion, the story of Icarus and Daedalus imparts essential lessons about hubris, balance, responsibility, self-awareness, and the complexities of freedom. By reflecting on these themes, we can navigate our ambitions with greater wisdom, ensuring that our pursuits enrich our lives rather than lead to our downfall.

“Pandora’s Box” – The Greek myth about the origin of human suffering and hope, tied to curiosity and consequence.

Pandora, gifted a sealed box by the gods, opens it out of curiosity. The box releases all human miseries but retains hope, symbolizing that even amid suffering, hope persists.

I

In realms where silent deities weave dreams,

And twilight’s breath veils mortal eyes in gray,

A myth unfolds beneath the starry beams,

Where fate entwines in cosmos' grand ballet.

On Olympus, where shadows waltz in trance,

And stardust mingles with the past’s old hues,

A vessel forged in twilight’s fleeting dance,

Conceals the threads where fate and time infuse.

To Pandora came a gift of dusky grace,

A box from night’s ephemeral embrace,

A crafted shell where timeless fates interlace,

A dance of gods in silent, mystic place.

Her hands, though tender, bore the weight of lore,

A vessel sealed with whispers of the dusk,
A silent hymn where dark and light implore,
The essence of the realms both vast and husk.

II

The gods, in wisdom cloaked in veiled delight,
Presented her this vessel, cold and steep,
"Beware," they whispered through the shadowed night,
"For in its depths, all mortal sorrows sleep."
Yet driven by a thirst both fierce and wild,
Pandora's trembling hands defied the fates,
The lid, a threshold where the shadows smiled,
Unleashed the grief that timeless wrath creates.
A storm surged forth, where sorrow's tempest roared,
A deluge from the ages dark and deep,
The gods' own curses through their anger poured,
Unleashed a realm where endless sorrows creep.
Disease and famine, war and blighted time,
Each curse a chain upon the soul's frail seam,
And man, ensnared in darkness' endless climb,
Found no reprieve within the shadowed dream.
Yet from the chasm where the shadows roared,
A single ember's fragile glow emerged,

A spark amid the void where darkness poured,

A beacon through the tempest's fierce converged.

This tender light, though faint and scarcely seen,

Glimmered within the heart of ceaseless gloom,

A symbol where despair and hope convene,

A whisper in the dark, a fleeting bloom.

III

In starkest revelation, cold and clear,

The box lay open, silence vast and deep,

A symbol of the gods' own harsh veneer,

And mankind's fate with sorrow's chains allied.

Pandora wept, her tears like tempest's breath,

The earth now bore the weight of ancient pain,

The gods, aloof, with distant, stern bequest,

Watched man embrace his grief's enduring chain.

In this crucible where shadows blend and wane,

The essence of mankind was sharply shown,

The gods' own gift, a trial to constrain,

Yet hope's own ember in the dark was sown.

A paradox where light and dark entwine,

A truth revealed in suffering's cruel dance,

That even in despair, hope shall refine,

A glimmer in the night's eternal trance.

Yet in the realm where light and darkness blend,

The gods' own schemes unravel, twist, and play,

For mortal hearts in shadowed depths transcend,

Their hopes entwined in both the night and day.

Pandora's plight, a tale of fate's own jest,

Where every curse bears seeds of future bloom,

In sorrow's depths, the echoes still attest,

And from the ashes rises life's new loom.

From ages past, the whispers softly rise,

Through time's long corridors, the legends spin,

A gift entwined with fate, a rift, a guise,

In mortal hearts, where timeless shadows grin.

The box of woes, a curse and boon combined,

A symbol of the gods' own fickle grace,

Where in the dark, a glimmer still aligned,

The light of hope in every darkened space.

As mankind wrestles with the gods' own jest,

And trials test the mettle of the soul,

A deeper truth through suffering's unrest,

Reveals the hidden path to make them whole.

In every curse, a spark of hope resides,

A whisper in the void, a faint reply,

For through the dark, the truth and light collide,

And in the night, new dreams begin to fly.

IV

SO PONDER WELL THIS myth of cosmic sweep,

In mortal hearts where echoes softly blend,

That from our trials, both bitter and deep,

A glimmering hope may yet its way send.

Curiosity, though it unveils the dark,

Can spark a flame that through the void will soar,

And in our suffering, where shadows mark,

A fleeting hope endures forevermore.

Thus tread with care through realms of light and shade,

And face the gods' own gifts with tempered grace,

For in the heart of chaos, fierce and laid,

There lies a truth no time can e'er erase.

From ancient lore, the gods' own tales unfold,

A mythic chronicle through ages bold,

Of mortal hearts that wrestle fate's cruel hand,

And find in darkness, light's most subtle strand.

Through every trial, the truth remains the same,

In suffering's embrace, we kindle flame.

So let this myth, through time, its echoes send,

A timeless hope that darkness cannot bend.

And through the ages, as the tales are spun,

The myth of Pandora's box is never done,

For in the dark, where hope and shadows meet,

A light persists, both fierce and bittersweet.

LIFE LESSONS

The story of Pandora's Box is a rich Greek myth that explores profound themes of curiosity, consequence, suffering, and hope. This tale offers several important life lessons that continue to resonate with us today.

At its core, the myth illustrates the dangers of curiosity. Pandora, created by the gods, is given a box (or jar) with strict instructions not to open it. However, her overwhelming curiosity leads her to disobey this command, resulting in disastrous consequences. This teaches us that while curiosity can be a driving force for discovery and understanding, it can also lead to unintended harm. The lesson here is to approach our curiosities with caution and to be aware of the potential risks that come with exploring the unknown.

The act of opening Pandora's box unleashes all the evils into the world—suffering, disease, and despair. This aspect of the story highlights the concept of consequence. Every action we take can have far-reaching effects, and it's crucial to consider the possible outcomes of our choices. Pandora's mistake serves as a reminder that not all knowledge is beneficial, and some truths may come at a high price. We learn to weigh our decisions carefully and consider how they might impact ourselves and others.

However, amidst the chaos and suffering unleashed from the box, hope remains trapped inside. This pivotal element of the story underscores the idea that hope is essential for human resilience. Even when faced with adversity and despair, hope provides a crucial lifeline. It encourages us to persevere through difficult times, reminding us that challenges are often temporary and that a brighter future is possible. This lesson teaches us that while we may encounter hardship, hope can inspire us to keep moving forward.

Furthermore, Pandora's Box reflects the complex nature of human existence. Life is filled with both joy and suffering, and the myth suggests that these elements are intertwined. Understanding that suffering is a part of life can help us cultivate empathy for others and appreciate moments of happiness more deeply. This duality encourages us to embrace the full spectrum of human experience, recognizing that both pain and joy contribute to our growth.

The story of Pandora's Box imparts valuable lessons about curiosity, the consequences of our actions, the importance of hope, and the complexity of human existence. By reflecting on these themes, we can navigate our lives with greater awareness, understanding that our choices can shape not only our own destinies but also the world around us. Ultimately, the myth serves as a reminder that even in the face of suffering, hope can light the way toward healing and renewal.

"The Trojan Horse" – The clever ruse that led to the fall of Troy, exploring themes of deception and fate.

This poem, "The Trojan Horse," explores the themes of deception, ambition, and the tragic consequences of war through the lens of the Trojan myth. It begins by setting the scene of Troy's proud yet doomed fate and unfolds the cunning plot of the Greeks, culminating in the moment of betrayal. As chaos ensues, the poem reflects on the choices that shape destinies, ultimately serving as a poignant reminder of the intertwined nature of fate and human ambition.

I

In ancient realms where legends intertwine,

Beneath the shadowed walls of fate divine,

Troy stood proud, a jewel in fate's cruel hand,

A beacon bright, yet lost in ambition's demand.

For ten long years, the clash of spears rang,

Valor and sorrow in the heart of war sang.

Under twilight's veil, whispers of fate spun,

As lovers and warriors faced what was begun.

The Greeks, with cunning, wove a dark design,

A wooden beast, a gift cloaked in a sign.

Odysseus, whose eyes mirrored the moon's deceit,

Conceived this ruse, his heart a paradox, bittersweet.

"Let them rejoice," he murmured in the night,

While shadows gathered, obscuring the light.

With fate's cruel smile, they plotted their course,

For in man's breast dwells ambition's treacherous force.

II

The Trojans, weary from the long siege of time,

Sought solace in victory, a rhythm, a rhyme.

They wheeled the horse through their gates of pride,

Blind to the specter that stirred deep inside.

With laughter and feasting, they welcomed their plight,

As dreams of tomorrow danced in the night.

But destiny whispered, veiled in a shroud,

A silence profound amidst the reveling crowd.

In shadows concealed, brave warriors thrived,

Hearts pulsing strong, with cunning revived.

The night thickened as the moon dimmed its glow,

They readied their souls for the depths of woe.

With breath held tight, they slipped from their cage,

The moment arrived to unleash the rage.

The gates of Troy opened, a Pandora's embrace,

In the twilight of trust, they unveiled their disgrace.

As dawn unfurled its pale fingers of light,

The walls echoed songs of a city in plight.

Swords gleamed like stars, both radiant and cold,

While whispers of ghosts through the corridors rolled.

Cassandra wept softly, her visions in vain,

Foretelling the doom wrapped in valor's disdain.

Yet as shadows converged, a fierce light arose,

In betrayal's embrace, a deeper truth grows.

III

Amidst the tumult, where honor once stood,

The sacred fell silent, now drenched in blood.

Odysseus, a figure cloaked in the fray,

Bore witness to sorrow as night swallowed day.

"Brothers, rise!" he called, as chaos unfurled,

"Let the dawn of our deeds be forever twirled!"

But the cries of the innocent rang through the air,

A requiem forged in the fires of despair.

Flames danced higher, consuming their pride,

As Troy, once a beacon, in ashes now died.

The fabric of fate unraveled, threadbare,

Entwining the brave with the weight of despair.

Each clash of steel echoed a sorrowful song,

Reminding us all where we once did belong.

In echoes of triumph, the shadows stood tall,

A testament written to the rise and the fall.

In the heart of the storm, where destinies clash,

The choices we make may lead to our ash.

In every heartbeat, in every brave stand,

Lies the weight of the world in the palm of a hand.

So, with every sword drawn, let us tread with care,

For the end of our journey can hang in the air.

IV

When dust settles softly on history's thread,

And the world reflects on the dreams that are dead,

What lessons emerge from the embers of Troy?

What truths linger long after glory's coy?

For fate weaves its patterns with strands of the heart,

Every great hero must play their own part.

In love and in loss, in laughter and tears,

We find in our journeys the echoes of years.

Let us remember the Trojan deceit,

The price of ambition, the sorrow of defeat.

For within every ruse lies a truth to be known:

That wisdom and folly together have grown.

As we walk through shadows in light's gentle gleam,

Let us choose with intention, and dare to dream.

The story of Troy is a mirror we face,

A reminder that fate and our choices embrace.

LIFE LESSONS

The story of the Trojan Horse is a powerful tale from Greek mythology that illustrates critical life lessons about deception, strategy, and the nature of fate. At its heart, the myth highlights the complexities of human behavior and the consequences of our actions.

One of the primary lessons from the Trojan Horse is the importance of deception and cunning. The Greeks, unable to breach the formidable walls of Troy after a long siege, devised a clever ruse involving a giant wooden horse. This strategy exemplifies how intelligence and creativity can triumph over brute force. It teaches us that sometimes, strategic thinking and clever planning can achieve what strength alone cannot. This lesson is particularly relevant in our lives, as we often face challenges that require innovative solutions rather than straightforward confrontation.

Additionally, the story underscores the theme of trust and betrayal. The Trojans, believing the Greeks had retreated, welcomed the horse into their city as a token of victory. This act of misplaced trust ultimately leads to their downfall. The myth serves as a reminder to be cautious about whom we trust and to critically assess situations before acting. It highlights the necessity of discernment in our relationships and decisions, as well as the potential consequences of naivety.

The fall of Troy also delves into the idea of fate and destiny. Despite the Trojans' initial confidence, their fate is sealed by their own actions and choices. The story suggests that while we may strive for control over our destinies, external forces and unforeseen consequences can drastically alter our paths. This duality invites reflection on the balance between agency and fate, urging us to be mindful of how our decisions can lead to unintended outcomes.

Moreover, the tale speaks to the theme of the consequences of pride. The Trojans' hubris in believing they had defeated the Greeks and their failure to recognize the potential threat of the horse illustrates how arrogance can blind us to reality. This lesson serves as a caution against overconfidence and encourages humility. Acknowledging our vulnerabilities can help us navigate challenges more effectively and remain open to new perspectives.

In summary, the story of the Trojan Horse imparts significant lessons about deception, trust, fate, and the dangers of pride. By examining these themes, we can better understand the complexities of human nature and the intricate web of choices that shape our lives. The myth serves as a reminder that intelligence and discernment are vital in navigating the challenges we face, and that even in moments of triumph, we must remain vigilant to the potential for unforeseen consequences. Ultimately, the story encourages us to embrace a balanced approach to ambition and humility, recognizing that both can coexist in our pursuit of success.

“Narcissus and Echo” – The myth of a man who falls in love with his reflection, and a nymph who can only repeat what she hears.

The poem "Narcissus and Echo" retells the myth of Narcissus, a young man entranced by his own reflection in a stream, and Echo, a nymph doomed to repeat the words of others. Set in a lush, magical glade, the poem explores themes of beauty, longing, and unrequited love. As Narcissus becomes increasingly consumed by his own image, he remains oblivious to Echo's deep affection, leading to her despair. Ultimately, his self-obsession results in tragedy, transforming him into a flower while Echo fades into a whisper. The poem serves as a poignant reminder of love, loss, and the dangers of vanity.

I

In a glade where sunlight wove through trembling leaves,

Where whispers danced with shadows that the heart believes,

There flowed a stream, crystalline as a dream's embrace,

Its surface held secrets, a delicate face.

Upon its banks, Narcissus stood, beauty laid bare,

Lost in the stillness, unaware of the prayer.

His laughter rang out, a melody bright and free,

A spirit unbound, basking in ecstasy.

Yet fate, with fingers of silver-threaded woe,

Wove tales of longing where shadows would grow.

Echo, a nymph, whose voice trailed like the breeze,
Could only repeat what the world would seize.
In her heart bloomed a love, tender as dawn's first light,
For the boy whose beauty would soon fade from sight.
But in her gaze, a sorrowful ache took flight,
For the love she could offer was swallowed by night.

II

One fateful day, as the sun dipped low and shy,
Narcissus wandered where wildflowers lie.
The nymph, in silence, beheld his fair face,
Her heart stirred with longing, a yearning embrace.
"Who calls?" he spoke, as the air trembled slight,
For Echo's voice rang back, a tender delight.
"Who calls?" she echoed, in soft, breathless sighs,
While he, lost in reverie, gazed at the skies.
Yet deeper than beauty, a mirror would show,
The flaw in his heart, an echo of woe.
He knelt by the stream, entranced by the sight,
A visage so lovely, it stole away light.
His heart caught in rapture, unknowing the chain,
While Echo, unseen, felt the sting of her pain.
"Who loves?" he pondered, his voice a sweet balm,

And the nymph whispered back, "Who loves?" in the calm.

Each day, he returned to the shimmering glass,

To gaze at the beauty that none could surpass.

But Echo, a shadow, grew faint in her guise,

As the flame of her passion turned cold in his eyes.

"Love me," she whispered, yet he could not hear,

For he drowned in reflection, blind to her tear.

With each soft reply, his heart turned to stone,

In the depths of his beauty, he stood all alone.

III

Then came the moment, as twilight drew near,

When the waters sparkled, revealing the fear.

He reached for his image, a longing to clasp,

But the water slipped through, a cruel, fleeting gasp.

"Why cannot you love me?" echoed her plea,

As Narcissus faltered, caught in destiny.

"Who loves?" he demanded, his voice taut with grief,

"Who loves?" whispered Echo, a heart wrought with belief.

But his heart had surrendered to hollow delight,

While Echo's spirit dimmed, lost to the night.

In that haunted stillness, a silence profound,

Both beauty and sorrow entwined, tightly wound.

With a shattering gasp, he fell to despair,

For the love he sought was forever elsewhere.

His heart, now a shadow, dissolved in the stream,

A reflection of sorrow, a fragmented dream.

In that instant, the gods, with a pitying gaze,

Watched the fate of a youth in a blinding haze.

With a flick of their fingers, a change was bestowed,

For Narcissus faded, his glory erode.

As petals drifted, a flower took root,

A symbol of beauty, its essence acute.

And Echo, in shadows, became but a sigh,

A voice in the distance, a lover's goodbye.

IV

So, remember the tale of Narcissus's plight,

A dance with reflection, consumed by the light.

For in searching for beauty, he lost all he knew,

And in the depths of his heart, love's echo withdrew.

The mirror may glimmer, but the heart must engage,

For love is a fire, not bound to a cage.

In silence, we hear the whispers of fate,

A reminder that love must not hesitate.

Let not your gaze linger too long on the shore,

For the waters may trick you, leaving you wanting more.

In the depths of your soul, let the echoes be clear,

For love finds its voice when we choose to draw near.

Thus, in the shadows of longing and grace,

We discover the beauty of love's true embrace.

LIFE LESSONS

The myth of Narcissus and Echo is a poignant tale that explores themes of self-love, the nature of communication, and the consequences of obsession. Through the tragic stories of Narcissus, who becomes infatuated with his own reflection, and Echo, who can only repeat the words of others, we glean valuable life lessons that resonate deeply in our contemporary lives.

One of the primary lessons from this myth is the danger of excessive self-love and narcissism. Narcissus's obsession with his own reflection ultimately leads to his downfall. His inability to look beyond himself prevents him from forming genuine connections with others. This aspect of the story serves as a cautionary tale about the pitfalls of vanity and self-absorption. It reminds us that while self-love is important, it must be balanced with empathy and an appreciation for others. True fulfillment comes not just from self-admiration but from meaningful relationships and connections with those around us.

Additionally, the character of Echo highlights the consequences of inadequate communication and the impact of unrequited love. Echo, cursed to repeat only what others say, symbolizes the struggles many face in expressing their true feelings and desires. Her longing for Narcissus, who is oblivious to her affection, reflects the pain of unreciprocated love and the difficulty of being heard. This aspect of the myth teaches us the importance of authentic communication in relationships. Being able to express ourselves and listen to others is essential for fostering understanding and intimacy.

Furthermore, the myth underscores the theme of identity and self-awareness. Narcissus's fixation on his reflection suggests a superficial understanding of self. He fails to recognize the value of who he is beyond his appearance. This serves as a reminder for us to cultivate a deeper sense of self that goes beyond physical attributes. Engaging in self-reflection and understanding our values and motivations can lead to a more fulfilling life, allowing us to connect with others on a more meaningful level.

Moreover, the tragic ending of the story highlights the consequences of disconnection and isolation. Narcissus ultimately loses everything due to his self-centeredness, while Echo fades away, leaving only her voice behind. This illustrates the importance of nurturing relationships and being present for those we care about. Isolation, whether from self-absorption or poor communication, can lead to loneliness and despair.

In summary, the myth of Narcissus and Echo offers profound lessons about the balance between self-love and empathy, the significance of authentic communication, the importance of self-awareness, and the dangers of isolation. By reflecting on these themes, we can navigate our relationships and personal growth with greater awareness, ensuring that we remain connected to ourselves and to others. The story serves as a timeless reminder that love, both for oneself and for others, requires a delicate balance to thrive.

"The Minotaur and the Labyrinth" – Theseus' journey into the labyrinth to defeat the Minotaur, symbolizing struggle and heroism.

This poem recounts the myth of Theseus and the Minotaur, set in ancient Crete. Theseus, a brave hero, volunteers to enter the labyrinth, a maze designed to imprison the fearsome Minotaur—a creature half-man, half-bull. The Minotaur symbolizes the darkness within human nature, while the labyrinth represents the complex journey of self-discovery and struggle. As Theseus confronts the beast, he is guided by Ariadne's thread, a symbol of hope and guidance. Ultimately, the poem explores themes of heroism, the duality of man, and the quest for identity amid chaos, reflecting the timeless battle between light and darkness.

I

In the shadowed realm where daylight wanes,

A labyrinth of sorrow coils and strains,

Where echoes whisper tales of dread and fate,

And heroes tread with hearts both brave and straight.

The Minotaur, a beast of dual birth,

Stands guardian of both despair and mirth,

A creature born from passion's fierce embrace,

In tangled corridors, he hides his face.

Amidst these walls, where hope and fear entwine,

Theseus, the bold, with heart and mind divine,

Steps forth, a spark against the gathering night,

With courage drawn from dreams of ancient light.

Oh labyrinth, your winding paths confound,

Yet in your depths, the echoes of souls resound,

Here, fate awaits, like shadows cast by flame,

Each turn a whisper, calling forth a name.

II

With ball of thread, a lifeline to his will,

Theseus descends, where time stands still,

Each footfall speaks of lives entwined in lore,

Of whispered vows and battles fought before.

In quiet corners, he can hear the sighs

Of those who wandered here, beneath dark skies,

They, too, had sought the truth, the light, the grace,

Yet found instead the silence of this place.

The Minotaur waits, a heart wrapped tight in pain,

A child of rage, of love, of loss, and gain,

He roams the maze, both monster and a man,

His roar a cry, for kindness never ran.

Theseus, with sword drawn, feels the tremor near,

A clash of destinies, a dance of fear,

Will he, the hero, claim his righteous prize,

Or find within the labyrinth his own demise?

III

As steel meets horn, the air ignites with strife,

A battle waged not just for breath, but life,

Theseus, in fury, strikes with valor's grace,

Yet in the beast's wild eyes, he sees his face.

A mirror held to all his doubts and dreams,

For in the Minotaur, his anguish teems,

Both bound to fate, yet yearning to be free,

Two souls entwined in tragic symmetry.

With every thrust, a question hangs in air:

What makes a hero? Is it strength, or care?

In grappling shadows, wisdom comes to light,

To conquer all the darkness, one must fight.

But in this clash of sinew, heart, and bone,

He finds that every victory feels alone,

And as the beast falls, crumpling to the ground,

A silence follows, deep and profound.

IV

In the stillness, Theseus stands, a king unmade,

For what is triumph, when the price is laid?

He wanders back, through corridors of dread,

A thread of sorrow in his heart now bred.

The labyrinth's whispers, like a haunting song,

Remind him that in triumph, we can wrong,

The Minotaur, a shadow of his own,

A beast of burdens that he cannot disown.

As light breaks forth, dispelling shades of night,

He carries with him the echoes of the fight,

For in the depths, he learned what none could teach:

That every battle fought is but a reach.

Through struggle, truth emerges, veiled in grief,

A hero's path is woven through belief.

So let us tread with care where shadows play,

For in the labyrinth, we find our way.

LIFE LESSONS

The story of the Minotaur and the Labyrinth is a compelling myth that encapsulates themes of struggle, heroism, and the journey toward self-discovery. As Theseus embarks on his quest to confront the Minotaur, he encounters profound life lessons that resonate with the human experience.

One of the most significant lessons from this tale is the importance of courage in the face of fear. The Minotaur, a monstrous creature dwelling in the labyrinth, symbolizes the fears and challenges that often seem insurmountable. Theseus's decision to enter the labyrinth despite the danger highlights the necessity of confronting our fears head-on. This lesson encourages us to embrace courage and face our own "monsters," whether they are personal doubts, external challenges, or difficult situations. By doing so, we can discover our strength and resilience.

Another key lesson is the value of strategy and intelligence in overcoming obstacles. The labyrinth itself represents complexity and confusion, illustrating that life's challenges can often feel disorienting. Theseus's reliance on Ariadne's thread to navigate the labyrinth emphasizes the importance of having a plan and utilizing resources wisely. This teaches us that while bravery is essential, it must be paired with thoughtful strategy. Life often requires a combination of courage and careful planning to navigate its twists and turns successfully.

The myth also speaks to the theme of self-discovery and transformation. As Theseus confronts the Minotaur, he undergoes a significant personal journey. The act of facing the creature becomes a metaphor for facing one's inner struggles and evolving in the process. This aspect of the story reminds us that confronting our fears can lead to profound personal growth. Through struggle, we often gain deeper insights into ourselves and our capabilities.

Furthermore, the story highlights the importance of help and collaboration. Theseus does not face the labyrinth alone; he receives guidance from Ariadne, who provides him with the means to navigate the maze. This underscores the value of seeking help and recognizing that we do not have to face our challenges in isolation. Building a support network can be crucial in overcoming obstacles, as others can offer insights and resources that enhance our journey.

Finally, the story of the Minotaur and the Labyrinth illustrates the notion of sacrifice and responsibility. Theseus takes on the role of a hero not just for personal glory, but to save others from the Minotaur's terror. This selflessness reflects the idea that true heroism involves responsibility toward others. By stepping into danger for the sake of those in need, Theseus embodies the qualities of a true leader, reminding us of the importance of considering the welfare of others in our actions.

In summary, the myth of the Minotaur and the Labyrinth imparts valuable lessons about courage, strategy, self-discovery, collaboration, and responsibility. By reflecting on these themes, we can navigate our own labyrinths with greater awareness and purpose, finding strength in our struggles and the wisdom to overcome the challenges we face. The journey toward heroism is not just about defeating external foes, but also about conquering our internal battles and growing through the experience.

“King Midas and the Golden Touch” – The cautionary tale of King Midas, whose greed led to ruin when everything he touched turned to gold.

This poem narrates the tale of King Midas, a ruler whose insatiable greed leads him to wish that everything he touches turns to gold. Initially reveling in his newfound power, Midas soon faces dire consequences when he realizes that even food and loved ones become lifeless gold at his touch. Stricken by regret, he seeks a way to reverse the curse. Eventually, he learns humility and the true value of life and love. The myth serves as a cautionary tale about the dangers of greed and the importance of appreciating what truly matters beyond material wealth.

I

In ancient realms where whispers weave through trees,

And golden light spills soft on whispered breeze,

There lived a king, adorned in wealth's embrace,

With eyes that glimmered like the sun’s warm grace.

Midas, sovereign of the golden throne,

In marble halls where treasures overgrown,

A heart ensnared by gleaming golden chains,

Ignored the echo of more tender gains.

His kingdom thrived, yet hunger stirred within,

A void unfilled by gold's seductive din.

For every bauble shone with hollow gleam,

And love, like shadow, fled from his bright dream.

In twilight's hush, when silence held the night,

His heart would yearn for solace from the light.

Yet vanity, like ivy, climbed his soul,

Till whispers turned to shouts, and lost control.

II

One fateful morn, the god of wine appeared,

With laughter laced in nectar, sweet and clear.

"Choose wisely, King, for all that glitters gold,

May hide the pain that silent hearts unfold."

With fervent wish, Midas reached for more,

"Let every touch turn gold, a wealth to soar!"

In haste, he claimed the boon, the pact was sealed,

Yet little did he know what fate revealed.

At first, the joy of golden touch was bliss,

Each simple thing transformed to gleaming kiss.

The fruits of earth, in gilded splendor glowed,

While treasures piled, and fortunes overflowed.

But soon the laughter turned to cries of dread,

For every morsel, every flower bred

A cursed fate, where joy began to wane,

And gold became a chain that bore his pain.

His daughter, fair, with laughter like the sun,

Embraced him once, then turned to stone, undone.

He reached for love, his hands met cold despair,

In gilded dreams, he found his heart laid bare.

"Is gold the worth of all that I have lost?"

He pondered deeply, feeling love's high cost.

Yet greed, a shadow, whispered in his ear,

"More gold, more power, cast away your fear!"

III

With frantic heart, he sought the god divine,

To plead for mercy, to undo the sign.

"Bacchus, hear me! I am but a fool,

For in my greed, I played the selfish rule."

The god appeared, with wisdom in his gaze,

"To know the worth of love, one must feel blaze.

Let go the chains that bind you to the gold,

Embrace the warmth of love that can't be sold."

With trembling hands, Midas touched the stream,

The water flowed, a glistening golden dream.

But in its depths, a truth began to rise,

That love, not gold, brings light to weary skies.

He washed away the curse, the golden touch,

And felt the world anew, a softer clutch.

His daughter's warmth returned, with laughter bright,

A lesson learned in shadows turned to light.

IV

Now in the garden where his heart once strayed,

Midas walked free, in love's embrace displayed.

He learned that riches bloom in bonds we share,

And not in gilded trinkets, rich and rare.

With every step, he felt the earth's kind grace,

In simple joys, he found his rightful place.

For life is more than treasures made of gold,

It's warmth of love and stories yet untold.

So raise a cup, and let the echoes ring,

In every heart, let love be the true king.

For Midas learned that wisdom, like the sun,

Is found in moments shared, and not in one.

LIFE LESSONS

The story of King Midas and the Golden Touch is a timeless cautionary tale that explores the dangers of greed and the true value of what we cherish in life.

Through Midas's journey, we glean several important life lessons that resonate with contemporary society.

At the heart of the tale is the theme of greed. King Midas's insatiable desire for wealth leads him to wish that everything he touched would turn to gold. While his wish is initially gratifying, it quickly spirals into a curse. This highlights the idea that unchecked greed can lead to destructive consequences. Midas's transformation from a wealthy king to a lonely figure unable to enjoy the simplest pleasures underscores the lesson that material wealth does not equate to happiness. In our lives, this serves as a reminder to seek balance and to appreciate what truly matters, rather than being consumed by the pursuit of riches.

Additionally, the story emphasizes the significance of contentment. Midas learns that true fulfillment comes not from accumulating wealth but from the relationships and experiences that enrich our lives. His inability to enjoy food, drink, and the warmth of human connection after his wish illustrates how greed can isolate us from the joys of life. This lesson encourages us to cultivate gratitude for what we have and to focus on the intangible treasures—love, friendship, and happiness—that cannot be quantified.

Another crucial lesson revolves around the idea of consequences. Midas's wish demonstrates that every action has repercussions, often unforeseen. When he realizes that his newfound ability is more of a curse than a blessing, he understands that our desires can lead to outcomes we never intended. This serves as a reminder to carefully consider the implications of our choices and to recognize that the path to fulfillment is often complex.

The tale also touches on the theme of humility. After experiencing the ramifications of his greed, Midas learns the value of humility and the importance of acknowledging our limitations. His journey from a greedy king to a humbled man illustrates that true wisdom comes from understanding that we are part of a larger community and that our actions affect those around us. Embracing humility can foster deeper connections and a greater appreciation for the contributions of others.

Finally, Midas's story culminates in a powerful lesson about redemption and change. After realizing the error of his ways, he seeks to reverse his wish. This act signifies the possibility of redemption and the opportunity for personal growth. It teaches us that, no matter how grave our mistakes, we can learn from them and strive to change for the better. The willingness to acknowledge our faults and seek improvement is a vital aspect of personal development.

In summary, the story of King Midas and the Golden Touch imparts essential lessons about greed, contentment, consequences, humility, and the potential for redemption. By reflecting on these themes, we can navigate our own lives with greater awareness, striving to prioritize the values that truly enrich our existence. Ultimately, the tale serves as a reminder that the pursuit of wealth should never overshadow the pursuit of happiness and meaningful relationships.

“The Sphinx’s Riddle” – The Greek myth of Oedipus solving the Sphinx’s riddle, focusing on knowledge and fate.

This poem explores the myth of Oedipus, a tragic figure from Greek mythology destined to confront a grim fate. As the King of Thebes, Oedipus seeks to save his city from a devastating plague. Guided by a prophecy, he must solve the riddle of the Sphinx, a monstrous creature that preys on travelers. The riddle—“What walks on four legs in the morning, two at noon, and three in the evening?”—symbolizes the stages of human life. Oedipus answers correctly, freeing Thebes but unwittingly sealing his own doom, as he later learns he has fulfilled the prophecy of patricide and incest.

I

In Thebes, where the sun bleeds gold at dusk,

A city wrapped in whispered fears and fate,

Where echoes of the past like shadows lurk,

The Sphinx, with cruel riddles, guards the gate.

Her wings outstretched, a darkened omen’s grace,

She perched above the stones of ancient lore,

With eyes like burning coals, a gaze that traced

The hearts of men, their dreams, and hopes, and more.

Here walked Oedipus, bold son of the soil,

With courage forged in steel, yet cloaked in doubt,

A seeker of the truth beneath the toil,
His thoughts a tempest, where all paths twist about.
What brings the dawn, yet fades with night's embrace?
What crawls on four, then two, then three in pain?
The riddle spun like threads in a fateful lace,
A tapestry of destiny's cruel chain.

II

The people wept beneath the Sphinx's reign,
Their harvests lost, their children gripped by dread,
In streets of gold, a hollow, aching pain,
Each whispered prayer a tear unshed, unsaid.
Oedipus, proud, with heart and mind ablaze,
Stepped forth to face the monster of the mind,
His thoughts a labyrinth, lost in darkened haze,
A mirror to his soul, a truth to find.
"Behold, ye trembling souls," he cried aloud,
"Fear not the beast that waits beyond the wall,
For in my heart, a spark shall pierce the shroud,
And cast aside the shadows, rise or fall."
Yet deep within, a war of thoughts unfurled,
A haunting echo of a prophecy,
A son destined to destroy his world,

To lay with kin and weave a tragedy.

The Sphinx, with laughter like a twisted breeze,

Responded with a smirk, her voice a hiss,

"Will you claim wisdom, brave one, with such ease?

What is the price for knowledge? What is bliss?"

Oedipus paused, the weight of fate a stone,

His hands clenched tight, a king beneath the crown,

What truth shall I uncover, all alone?

To seek the light, must I wear sorrow's gown?

III

He drew a breath, the moment heavy, still,

The riddle danced upon his lips like flame,

"Man is the creature who must bend to will,

A child in dawn, then strong, then frail—yet same."

With words like arrows, swift and keen, he struck,

The Sphinx recoiled, her laughter turned to woe,

In his triumph, the web of fate was plucked,

Yet in that victory, deeper shadows grow.

For what is victory when truth unveils

The hidden depths of darkness in the light?

Oedipus stood, his heart in tangled trails,

A king who wore his blindness, masked from sight.

The Sphinx dissolved in dust, her riddle solved,
But in its wake, a mirror turned on him,
As knowledge bloomed, the fate of all evolved,
He grasped a truth that dimmed his vision's whim.

IV

And thus he stood, the threads of fate entwined,
A man whose quest for truth bore bitter fruit,
The echoes of the Sphinx forever bind
His name to sorrow, in a tale acute.
Oedipus, the seeker, now revealed,
In seeking wisdom, found a tragic end,
For fate is woven tight, its fabric sealed,
In knowledge lies the path where shadows blend.
Yet let us ponder on this timeless plight,
For wisdom often wears a shroud of pain,
What is the cost of knowledge in the light?
To seek the truth, must one embrace the chain?
In every riddle lies a dual face,
Of knowledge and the price it bears in blood,
Oedipus, the king, now lost in space,
A tale of man and fate, forever flood.

LIFE LESSONS

The story of the Sphinx's riddle is a compelling narrative from Greek mythology, primarily associated with Oedipus, who confronts the Sphinx in order to save the city of Thebes. This myth explores profound themes related to knowledge, fate, and the consequences of human actions, offering several important life lessons.

One of the central lessons from this tale is the value of knowledge and wisdom. The Sphinx poses a riddle: "What walks on four legs in the morning, two legs at noon, and three legs in the evening?" Oedipus's ability to solve this riddle demonstrates the importance of critical thinking and problem-solving skills. This encourages us to seek knowledge actively and to use our intellect to navigate the challenges we face. In life, questions often arise that require us to think deeply and creatively, and Oedipus's success underscores the idea that knowledge can empower us to overcome obstacles.

The riddle also reflects the theme of human experience and the stages of life. The answer—humans, who crawl as infants, walk upright in adulthood, and use a cane in old age—symbolizes the journey of life. This teaches us to recognize and embrace the different phases of our existence. Understanding that life is a progression filled with growth, change, and ultimately vulnerability encourages us to appreciate each stage and the lessons it imparts. It invites reflection on how our experiences shape us and the importance of empathy for others at different points in their journeys.

Moreover, the story highlights the concept of fate and destiny. Oedipus's quest to defeat the Sphinx is intertwined with the larger narrative of his fate, as foretold by the oracle. This introduces the idea that while we may possess the ability to make choices and solve problems, our lives are also influenced by forces beyond our control. The interplay between fate and free will in Oedipus's story prompts us to reflect on the extent to which we can shape our destinies. It reminds us that, although we may strive to exert control over our lives, unforeseen events and circumstances can alter our paths.

Additionally, the resolution of the riddle and the defeat of the Sphinx brings about a sense of hubris and the consequences of overconfidence. Oedipus's triumph leads to a rapid rise in status, but this also foreshadows the tragic elements of his story. His confidence in solving the riddle may blind him to the warnings about his fate. This serves as a caution against arrogance, illustrating that while self-assurance is necessary, it should be tempered with humility and awareness of potential pitfalls.

In summary, the story of the Sphinx's riddle imparts essential lessons about the significance of knowledge, the journey of life, the interplay of fate and free will, and the dangers of hubris. By reflecting on these themes, we can better navigate our own lives, seeking wisdom, embracing the stages of our existence, and understanding the balance between striving for control and accepting the uncertainties that life presents. Ultimately, the myth serves as a reminder that knowledge is a powerful tool, but it must be wielded with humility and respect for the greater forces at play in our lives.

“Thor and the Midgard Serpent” – The Norse god Thor’s epic battle with Jörmungandr, symbolizing struggle against overwhelming odds.

In Norse mythology, Thor, the god of thunder, faces Jörmungandr, the Midgard Serpent, a colossal creature that encircles the Earth. This epic confrontation symbolizes the struggle between order and chaos. The gods fear Jörmungandr, as its presence threatens their realm. In a climactic battle, Thor wields his mighty hammer, Mjölnir, determined to defeat the serpent. Their clash is not just a physical confrontation; it reflects deeper themes of fate, knowledge, and the inevitable cycles of life and death. Ultimately, Thor’s struggle against Jörmungandr foreshadows the larger cataclysmic events of Ragnarok, highlighting the tragic inevitability of destiny.

I

In ancient realms where shadows weave and sigh,

Where frost-tinged mountains pierce the dusky sky,

Thor, son of Odin, with heart like the sun,

Walked pathways of the gods, where battles were won.

Midgard lay beneath, a realm of mortal toil,

While whispers of Jörmungandr, the serpent, coil.

Legends told of a creature born of the sea,

A harbinger of doom, fierce and wild, yet free.

In twilight's embrace, beneath the waning light,

The skies brewed a storm, heralding the fight.

As fate spun its web, weaving threads of the past,

Thor felt the weight of destiny, grim and vast.

II

From Asgard's throne to the shores of Midgard's plight,

He strode, wielding Mjölnir, his hammer of might.

With courage unfurled like banners in the gale,

He sought the great serpent, the bringer of wail.

Legends whispered of prophecies long foretold,

Of battles unending, of heroes grown bold.

In taverns and halls, the sagas would echo,

Of Thor's fated clash, of glory and woe.

But deep in his heart, a shadow took root,

A doubt, like a thorn, wrapped tight at its root.

"Am I but a pawn in fate's cruel design?

Will my strength alone break the serpent's spine?"

With each step, the earth trembled beneath his tread,

As whispers of fear danced, and courage bled.

He faced the horizon where the waters met night,

A shimmering veil of fate, twisted and tight.

Jörmungandr's form, like a tempest unleashed,

Risen from depths where the ancients had feasted.

With scales like the moonlight, reflecting the stars,
The serpent coiled tight, bearing wisdom and scars.
"Thor, why do you seek the end of your kin?
What price will you pay for the strength within?"
His voice echoed darkly, a haunting refrain,
"Will victory's joy outweigh the weight of your pain?"

III

In the heart of the storm, where thunderbirds scream,
The clash of the titans shattered the dream.
Thor, with Mjölnir raised, a beacon of flame,
Met the serpent's gaze, unyielding, untame.
With each blow that fell, the heavens would crack,
As fate writhed in laughter, weaving destiny's track.
Lightning danced around them, fierce and alive,
As Thor struck with fury, determined to strive.
"Let the heavens witness this trial of might,
For in this confrontation, I'll claim back the light!"
Yet in the depths of battle, a whisper took flight,
A fleeting thought lingered, veiled in the night:
"What if strength is but folly, and wisdom a curse?
What if this struggle is but a reverse?"
As the tide of their struggle drew near to its close,

The serpent unfurled, its terrible pose.

With jaws that could swallow the sun and the moon,

It surged forth in fury, a storm in full bloom.

Thor felt the earth shift, his resolve turned to stone,

For in the face of the serpent, he stood all alone.

Yet as the final blow fell, he glimpsed the true cost—

The price of his glory, the friendships now lost.

The sky burned with fury as victory rang,

But echoes of doubt through the ages would hang.

"Is this what I sought, this triumph so stark?

A fleeting reflection, a voice in the dark?"

IV

Now resting in silence, the dust settles low,

Thor pondered the battle, the ebb and the flow.

In victory's shadow, what price did he pay?

The serpent lay vanquished, yet wisdom felt gray.

For knowledge is burden, a double-edged sword,

In seeking one truth, he'd left peace ignored.

With the weight of the heavens resting on his brow,

Thor learned that true strength lies not just in the now.

In the heart of the struggle, wisdom unfolds,

That might without mercy is but a tale told.

So he raised his gaze to the infinite skies,

And whispered a promise, with hope in his eyes.

"To battle is noble, but to understand,

Is the mightiest victory, a truth close at hand."

In echoes of thunder, the legends would sing,

Of Thor, the wise warrior, and the peace that he'd bring.

LIFE LESSONS

The story of Thor and the Midgard Serpent, Jörmungandr, is a powerful narrative from Norse mythology that encapsulates themes of struggle, bravery, and the confrontation of overwhelming odds. Through Thor's epic battle with the serpent, we glean important life lessons that resonate in various aspects of our lives.

One of the primary lessons from this myth is the value of courage in the face of adversity. Thor, the god of thunder, faces Jörmungandr, a colossal serpent that encircles the Earth. Despite the sheer size and power of the serpent, Thor does not back down. This teaches us that courage is essential when confronting our fears and challenges. In our lives, we often encounter situations that seem insurmountable, whether they are personal, professional, or existential. Thor's determination reminds us that true bravery is about facing these challenges head-on, even when the odds are stacked against us.

Another significant theme is the importance of perseverance. The battle between Thor and the Midgard Serpent is not just a physical confrontation; it represents the relentless struggle against formidable obstacles. Thor's determination to defeat Jörmungandr illustrates that success often requires sustained effort and resilience. This lesson encourages us to remain steadfast in our pursuits, even when we encounter setbacks or feel overwhelmed. It serves as a reminder that perseverance can lead to growth and eventual triumph.

The myth also speaks to the idea of accepting one's destiny. Thor's battle with Jörmungandr is prophesied, highlighting the inevitability of fate in Norse mythology. This aspect encourages us to recognize that some challenges are part of a larger narrative. Accepting our fate does not mean passivity; instead, it calls for an active engagement with the circumstances we face. By understanding that certain struggles are inherent to our journeys, we can approach them with a sense of purpose and resolve.

Furthermore, the story illustrates the concept of sacrifice. Thor's confrontation with the serpent requires immense strength and commitment. In life, we often face situations where achieving our goals necessitates personal sacrifices. This narrative encourages us to consider what we are willing to give up to overcome challenges or pursue our dreams. It teaches that while sacrifice may be painful, it is often a necessary component of growth and achievement.

Additionally, the relationship between Thor and Jörmungandr reflects the duality of good and evil. The serpent represents chaos and destruction, while Thor embodies order and protection. Their battle symbolizes the ongoing struggle between these forces in our lives. This lesson prompts us to consider how we engage with conflict and strive to maintain balance in the face of adversity. It encourages us to reflect on our values and the ways we can act with integrity in challenging situations.

The story of Thor and the Midgard Serpent imparts vital lessons about courage, perseverance, acceptance of destiny, sacrifice, and the duality of good and evil. By reflecting on these themes, we can better navigate our own struggles and challenges, drawing inspiration from Thor's unwavering determination and bravery. Ultimately, the myth serves as a reminder that while we may face overwhelming odds, our resolve and commitment can lead us to victory in our own battles.

"Ragnarök: The Twilight of the Gods" – The Norse myth of the end of the world, a battle between gods and giants, leading to rebirth.

In Norse mythology, Ragnarök marks the cataclysmic end of the world, a series of events culminating in a great battle between gods and giants. As the world faces chaos, the once harmonious realms descend into conflict. The fierce wolf Fenrir devours Odin, while Thor faces the Midgard Serpent, Jörmungandr, in a climactic struggle. Despite the gods' bravery, they fall, but from the ashes of destruction, a new world emerges, symbolizing rebirth and renewal. This myth reflects themes of fate, the cyclical nature of existence, and the inevitability of change, emphasizing that even in destruction, there is hope for renewal.

I

In ancient realms where whispers breathe the night,

Amidst the shadows of the frost-tinged trees,

The twilight gathered, draped in whispered fright,

As Loki's laughter danced upon the breeze.

The skies foretold of thunder's primal roar,

Of giants stirred from their eternal sleep,

While Asgard stood, a fortress evermore,

In glimmering gold, where valiant warriors weep.

Odin, the Allfather, with wisdom profound,

Sensed fate's approach, a shadow on the ground.

He gazed into the well where knowledge flows,
And saw the threads of destiny entwined;
The serpent coiled, its power in repose,
A harbinger of chaos, fate unkind.

II

From distant realms, the giants marched with ire,
With fiery breath and hearts of stone and frost,
They sought to claim the heavens, fueled by fire,
In thunder's clash, the lines of hope would cost.

The Valkyries flew with whispers of despair,
Bearing the souls of heroes to the hall,
Yet even they felt dread within the air,
As night encroached, threatening to enthrall.

Thor, with hammer raised, felt fury swell,
His heart a tempest, pounding like the sea,
He stood against the serpent, knew too well,
The cost of pride and strength's false certainty.

"Jörmungandr!" he roared, the waters churned,
"Come forth, and meet your end beneath my might!"
The world held breath, as destinies adjourned,
For battles writ in stars would soon ignite.

III

Upon the field where fire and ice entwined,

The clash of titans rang through realms of old,

With every strike, the fates of gods defined,

As echoes of the past began to unfold.

Jörmungandr writhed, a tempest born of hate,

Its scales, like shadows, glimmered in the night,

Thor's hammer fell, a force to challenge fate,

But darkness loomed, obscuring even light.

With every blow, the heavens trembled sore,

Yet as the serpent struck, the world went pale,

Thor felt the poison seep into his core,

And with each heartbeat, hope began to fail.

In final moments, fate entwined their souls,

The hammer's arc, a luminous embrace,

A clash of wills, as destiny unrolls,

Yet both would find their end in death's cold grace.

IV

But from the ashes, new worlds shall arise,

The cycle of existence ever turns,

For in destruction, life's true essence lies,

In hearts reborn, a flame that ever burns.

Odin's wisdom, in the silence speaks,

That life and death are threads of a grand weave,

In every loss, the spirit humbly seeks,

A deeper truth, a reason to believe.

So let us honor those who brave the storm,

For in their strife, the seeds of hope are sown;

In every battle fought, a spirit warm,

A testament that even gods atone.

Ragnarök, a tale of end and start,

In every ending, life's new journey lies;

Embrace the storm, for in the shadows' heart,

Awaits the dawn, where love and courage rise.

LIFE LESSONS

The myth of Ragnarök is a pivotal story in Norse mythology, detailing the apocalyptic battle between gods, giants, and various mythical creatures that ultimately leads to the destruction and rebirth of the world. This grand narrative imparts several profound life lessons that resonate with human experience, touching on themes of inevitability, transformation, and hope.

One of the most significant lessons from Ragnarök is the concept of inevitability and acceptance of fate. The events of Ragnarök are foretold, and despite the gods' power, they cannot escape their destined confrontation. This aspect of the myth teaches us that certain events in life are beyond our control. Learning to accept the inevitability of certain challenges or endings can foster resilience. Instead of resisting what we cannot change, we can focus on how we respond to these circumstances, understanding that acceptance can be a powerful step toward personal growth.

Another important theme is the idea of courage in the face of destruction. The gods, despite knowing that many will perish in the battle, confront their fates with bravery. This teaches us that courage is not the absence of fear but the willingness to face it head-on. In our own lives, we often encounter situations that seem catastrophic—loss, failure, or change. Ragnarök reminds us that, even in the darkest moments, we can summon the courage to face our challenges and stand for what we believe in.

The myth also emphasizes the theme of transformation and rebirth. After the devastation of Ragnarök, the world is reborn, symbolizing the cyclical nature of existence. This lesson highlights the idea that endings often lead to new beginnings. In life, we may face endings that feel overwhelming, but these can also be opportunities for renewal and growth. Embracing change, even when it is painful, can lead to new perspectives and possibilities. This aspect of the myth encourages us to view challenges as potential catalysts for transformation.

Moreover, Ragnarök reflects the interconnectedness of all beings. The battle involves not only gods and giants but also creatures and forces from all realms. This interconnectedness emphasizes that our actions can have far-reaching consequences. Understanding our place in a larger community encourages us to act with intention and responsibility. It reminds us that our choices can impact others, reinforcing the idea of collective fate and shared experiences.

Lastly, the story conveys a message of hope. Despite the destruction and chaos of Ragnarök, the myth concludes with a vision of a renewed world where survivors thrive in peace and harmony. This hopeful outlook inspires us to hold onto optimism, even in challenging times. It suggests that, although we may face trials and tribulations, there is always the potential for a brighter future. This lesson encourages us to cultivate resilience and maintain hope, as it can guide us through difficult periods and inspire us to work towards a better world.

In summary, the myth of Ragnarök imparts essential lessons about inevitability, courage, transformation, interconnectedness, and hope. By reflecting on these themes, we can better navigate our own life challenges, embracing change and finding strength in adversity. Ultimately, Ragnarök serves as a powerful reminder that even in the face of destruction, there is the possibility of renewal and a brighter tomorrow.

"The Valkyries" – Norse warrior maidens who choose who will live and die in battle, symbolizing destiny and bravery.

This poem explores the myth of the Valkyries, warrior maidens from Norse mythology tasked with choosing those who will live and die in battle. These fierce women, led by the goddess Freyja, guide fallen heroes to Valhalla, where they prepare for Ragnarok, the cataclysmic end of the world. Symbolizing destiny and bravery, the Valkyries embody the conflict between fate and free will, as they navigate the chaos of war and the inevitability of death. Their role highlights the honor and glory found in sacrifice, reflecting the complex relationship between mortality and valor in Norse culture.

I

In mist-cloaked realms where shadows play,

Amidst the echoing clang of fate,

The Valkyries soar, in twilight's gray,

Warrior maids, arbiters of state.

Their wings unfurl, a spectral dance,

Over battlefields where destinies collide,

Choosing the brave, bestowing a chance,

As the fallen gods in sorrow abide.

Beneath the sky of swirling ash,

The whispers of legends in twilight's breath,

A world on edge, poised for the crash,

Where valor and despair embrace in death.

Here the echoes of swords, like thunder, ring,

As giants stir in the shadows of night,

With courage woven in the hearts they bring,

To face the dusk, to challenge the light.

II

Odin's call, a clarion through the dark,

Summons his maidens, fierce and unbowed,

In shimmering armor, they ride, they spark,

The fierce fires of valor, proud and loud.

Each glance, a promise, each flight, a plea,

To honor the souls who dare to aspire,

For in their choice, the dance of destiny,

Burns with the passion of a purifying fire.

In the clash of blades, the cries arise,

Echoing tales of courage long gone,

The battle unfolds 'neath stormy skies,

As blood mingles with the dawn's first yawn.

Each warrior fights with a heart ablaze,

For in their struggle, a fate to unfold,

To carve their names in eternal praise,

In the annals of time, their stories told.

Yet whispers of doubt weave through the fray,

As the Valkyries ponder the cost of grace,

Is valor enough when shadows sway?

In the dance of death, who holds the place?

Each choice they make, a thread in the loom,

Weaving the fabric of fate's cruel jest,

For life and death in a moment bloom,

And honor lies heavy on each maiden's breast.

III

Then, through the storm, the giants roar,

Jörmungandr rises, serpent of doom,

A tide of darkness, a mythic lore,

Bringing forth chaos, sealing the tomb.

The Valkyries gather, their spirits entwined,

In the heart of the maelstrom, courage ignites,

With swords drawn high, and intentions aligned,

They charge forth, embodying the night.

In the fierce clash of steel and sinew,

The heavens tremble, stars dim with dread,

For each strike lands, the world anew,

As they dance with fate, where many have bled.

The earth shakes beneath the weight of their fight,

Each swing of their blades a poem of power,

In the light of the moon, shrouded in night,

They become the storm, the darkest hour.

IV

Yet in the wreckage, amidst the despair,

A glimmer of dawn peeks through the gloom,

For the Valkyries, brave, their hearts laid bare,

Find strength in their choices, amidst the tomb.

As the last giant falls, silence befalls,

And whispers of valor drift on the breeze,

In the wake of the battle, the courage calls,

To honor the lives, their memories seize.

So here in the echoes, their stories resound,

Of bravery woven in the fabric of fate,

For the Valkyries' choice, profound and unbound,

Crafts a legacy, a luminous state.

In the twilight of legends, their shadows will sway,

As warriors remember the battles they braved,

For in every ending, there lies a new day,

And through their courage, the world is saved.

LIFE LESSONS

The story of the Valkyries, the fierce warrior maidens of Norse mythology, offers rich insights into themes of destiny, bravery, and the complexity of choice. These figures, who select those worthy of honor and glory in battle, serve as powerful symbols of the interplay between fate and individual agency. From their tale, we can extract several important life lessons that resonate across cultures and time.

One significant lesson is the concept of destiny. The Valkyries are tasked with determining the fates of warriors, a role that highlights the idea that life and death are often beyond human control. This understanding encourages us to reflect on our own lives and the forces that shape our destinies. While we may strive for agency in our choices, recognizing that certain outcomes are predetermined can bring a sense of peace. Accepting that fate plays a role in our journeys allows us to focus on making the best choices within the parameters of our circumstances.

The Valkyries also exemplify bravery in various forms. Their role requires them to confront the chaos of battle and make difficult decisions about who lives and dies. This bravery is not only about physical strength but also about the moral courage to make choices that may lead to conflict or sadness. In our lives, we are often faced with situations that demand courage, whether in standing up for what we believe in or making tough decisions that affect ourselves and others. The Valkyries remind us that bravery comes in many forms and is essential for navigating life's complexities.

Moreover, the tale of the Valkyries speaks to the importance of honor and valor. The warriors they select are often those who demonstrate exceptional bravery and skill in battle. This emphasizes the value of living with integrity and striving for excellence in our endeavors. It encourages us to cultivate qualities such as resilience, dedication, and a commitment to our values, as these traits can lead to recognition and respect, not only from others but also within ourselves.

The Valkyries also represent the notion of sacrifice. Their decisions impact the lives of many, showcasing the idea that leadership and responsibility often come with significant burdens. In our lives, we may find ourselves in positions where our choices affect others, and understanding the weight of those choices can foster empathy and consideration. Recognizing that our actions can lead to both triumphs and losses helps us develop a sense of accountability.

Finally, the story of the Valkyries highlights the interplay between life and death. Their role in choosing the slain warriors for Valhalla reflects the cyclical nature of existence. This aspect encourages us to contemplate our own mortality and the legacies we wish to leave behind. It serves as a reminder to live fully, embracing each moment and striving to make a positive impact on the world around us.

In summary, the tale of the Valkyries imparts essential lessons about destiny, bravery, honor, sacrifice, and the balance between life and death. By reflecting on these themes, we can better navigate our own journeys, embracing the complexities of choice and the courage required to face life's challenges. Ultimately, the story encourages us to live with intention and integrity, recognizing that our paths are shaped by both our choices and the larger forces at play in our lives.

"Odin's Quest for Wisdom" – The story of the Norse god Odin sacrificing his eye at Mimir's well to gain wisdom.

This poem explores the Norse myth of Odin's quest for wisdom, centered around his sacrifice at Mimir's well. Odin, the All-Father and god of knowledge, seeks deeper understanding to navigate the complexities of fate and existence. To gain the wisdom of the ages, he willingly sacrifices one of his eyes, symbolizing the price of enlightenment. Mimir, the guardian of the well, grants him insight into the cosmos and the inevitable Ragnarok, the end of the world. This act of sacrifice reflects themes of destiny, the pursuit of knowledge, and the burdens that accompany great wisdom, highlighting the eternal quest for understanding.

I

In the shadowed realms where whispers dwell,

Amidst the ancient trees and the icy stream,

Odin roams, the All-Father, in search of the well,

Where Mimir's waters glisten, a dream within a dream.

The crows caw secrets from the heights of the pines,

While the wind carries tales of fates entwined,

In the tapestry of existence, where destiny aligns,

And the pulse of the cosmos is quietly enshrined.

The world is a fragile web, each thread a story spun,

Of valor, of loss, and the price of the wise;

In the heart of the storm, where the battles are won,

Wisdom beckons, a flame beneath starry skies.

Odin, with one eye cloaked in shadows profound,

Seeks knowledge beyond the reach of mortal men,

For wisdom is a path, where both light and dark abound,

A journey of sacrifice, an eternal requiem.

II

Through the misty valleys, where the ancient runes lie,

He wanders with purpose, his heart a restless flame,

For in the echoing silence, he hears the world's cry,

A call to the seeker, a summons to the game.

His breath is a whisper, as the earth turns cold,

And the spirits of yore dance in the twilight haze,

Each step a reminder of the stories untold,

Each shadow a memory of forgotten days.

He arrives at the well, where the roots intertwine,

Gnarled fingers of fate clutch the stones that gleam,

Mimir sits waiting, with wisdom divine,

Guarding the waters of memory's endless stream.

"Speak, All-Father," he murmurs, with eyes like the night,

"What is it you seek in the depths of this well?"

"To trade what is precious, to exchange for insight,

To grasp the eternal, to break wisdom's spell."

With a nod and a sigh, Odin lifts his sword high,

And in a flash of steel, he sacrifices sight,

The pain is a tempest, a howl in the sky,

Yet he embraces the darkness, for truth is his light.

In that moment of anguish, the cosmos unfurls,

Visions of ages cascade like a stream,

Of battles and glory, of love and of pearls,

The fabric of existence, woven into a dream.

III

As he drinks from the waters, the world shifts and sways,

Visions of giants and gods begin to entwine,

The threads of their fates, a complex ballet,

Revealing the shadows that linger in time.

He sees Baldr's bright laughter, cut short by despair,

The echoes of Ragnarok, where destinies clash,

In the furnace of chaos, where souls are laid bare,

And the flicker of hope is but a fleeting flash.

Yet wisdom is burdensome, a crown made of thorns,

For with each truth uncovered, a sorrow is born,

He feels the weight of existence, heavy and stark,

The laughter of mortals, now tinged with a mark.

Odin cries out, his voice a tempest's roar,

"Is knowledge a blessing or a curse I must bear?

In the halls of Valhalla, where warriors implore,

Does wisdom bring solace or deepen despair?"

The waters ripple softly, as Mimir's voice sighs,

"Wisdom is a mirror, reflecting all you seek,

In shadows and light, in the truth of the wise,

The path to enlightenment is seldom for the meek."

With this revelation, Odin's heart swells wide,

For wisdom is a journey, a dance with the unknown,

Each step a revelation, each tear a guide,

In the tapestry of life, we are never alone.

IV

Emerging from darkness, with his newfound sight,

Odin gazes upon the world with eyes of a sage,

The beauty and sorrow, a duality of light,

Each heartbeat a story, each moment a page.

He understands now, in the quiet of dawn,

That knowledge is a river, ever-flowing and deep,

A cycle of life, where endings are drawn,

And the promise of rebirth lies softly asleep.

In his heart, a fierce flame burns brighter than before,

For wisdom is woven in laughter and pain,

In the dance of creation, we are bound to explore,

Through loss and through longing, we find our refrain.

Odin, the seeker, now walks with the wise,

Embracing the shadows that teach us to see,

For in every sacrifice, the soul learns to rise,

In the quest for true wisdom, we set ourselves free.

LIFE LESSONS

Odin's quest for wisdom, marked by his sacrifice of an eye at Mimir's well, is a profound narrative in Norse mythology that imparts significant life lessons about the pursuit of knowledge, the nature of sacrifice, and the value of insight. This story emphasizes that wisdom often requires considerable personal cost and serves as a guide for navigating life's complexities.

One of the central lessons from Odin's journey is the importance of the pursuit of knowledge. Odin, revered as the god of wisdom and war, understands that true insight goes beyond mere information; it requires deep understanding and experience. His willingness to sacrifice his eye illustrates the lengths to which he is willing to go to gain profound knowledge. This teaches us that the quest for wisdom is a lifelong endeavor, one that demands dedication, humility, and an openness to learning. In our own lives, we should recognize that seeking knowledge can lead to personal growth and enlightenment, even when it involves challenges or discomfort.

The story also highlights the theme of sacrifice. Odin's choice to give up his eye symbolizes the idea that meaningful gains often come at a cost. This lesson encourages us to reflect on what we are willing to sacrifice for our goals and aspirations. Whether it be time, comfort, or even relationships, understanding that sacrifice is often part of achieving our dreams can help us prepare for the realities of pursuing our passions. It reminds us that the most valuable rewards usually require effort and sometimes painful choices.

Moreover, Odin's journey reflects the idea of perseverance in the face of adversity. The quest for wisdom is fraught with challenges, and Odin's determination to seek out Mimir's well exemplifies the resolve needed to overcome obstacles. In our lives, we may encounter setbacks or discouragement in our pursuit of knowledge or self-improvement. This narrative encourages us to remain steadfast and resilient, understanding that perseverance is key to unlocking deeper insights and personal growth.

Additionally, the tale underscores the interconnectedness of knowledge and experience. Odin's sacrifice grants him access to the well of wisdom, which contains not only information but also the experiences of the past. This highlights the idea that knowledge is not static; it is shaped by our experiences and the context in which we live. Embracing this interconnectedness encourages us to learn from our own experiences and those of others, fostering a more comprehensive understanding of the world around us.

Finally, Odin's quest emphasizes the significance of self-awareness and introspection. By sacrificing his eye, Odin acknowledges the limitations of perception and the importance of looking beyond the surface to gain true understanding. This encourages us to practice self-reflection and critical thinking in our own lives, urging us to question our assumptions and seek a deeper comprehension of our thoughts, feelings, and motivations.

In conclusion, Odin's quest for wisdom imparts essential lessons about the pursuit of knowledge, the necessity of sacrifice, perseverance, the interconnectedness of experience, and the importance of self-awareness. By reflecting on these themes, we can enhance our understanding of ourselves and the world, recognizing that the journey toward wisdom is both challenging and rewarding. Ultimately, Odin's story inspires us to embrace the complexities of life with curiosity and courage, understanding that the quest for knowledge is a noble and transformative endeavor.

“Beowulf and Grendel” – The Anglo-Saxon tale of the hero Beowulf’s battle with the monstrous Grendel, symbolizing heroism and fate.

This poem retells the epic tale of Beowulf, an Anglo-Saxon hero who confronts the monstrous creature Grendel, who terrorizes the mead hall of Heorot. Driven by a desire for glory and honor, Beowulf travels from his homeland to face Grendel, believing that his strength and courage will prevail. The story explores themes of heroism, fate, and the struggle between good and evil. In the climactic battle, Beowulf defeats Grendel by tearing off his arm, symbolizing the triumph of humanity over darkness. Ultimately, the poem reflects on the nature of bravery and the inevitable fate that awaits all heroes.

I

In shadowed halls where echoes weave and wane,

Beneath the pall of night, a kingdom lies,

Where ancient whispers stir in the cold, dark bane,

Of Grendel’s curse, a monster born from sighs.

In Heorot, brave hearts once laughed, now quake,

As shadows dance, and fate’s cruel jest unfolds,

With every death, the flames of hope forsake,

The light of dawn, where warrior dreams are sold.

The moon, a silver coin, spins tales of dread,

While restless spirits roam the misty glade,
And heroes wait with bated breath and lead,
For valor's test, a deadly masquerade.
Oft did they speak of glory, honor's call,
Yet in the silence, dread holds court supreme,
A haunting cry from darkened, endless hall,
The echo of a distant, broken dream.

II

Then came the tide, as Beowulf, bold and bright,
With strength like oak and courage forged in fire,
From Geatland's shores, a beacon in the night,
His heart aflame with destiny's desire.
He sought the beast, a specter of the night,
To cleanse the stain upon the warrior's creed,
With each footfall, he stirred the ancient fight,
The tale of fate, in blood and glory, freed.
Through marshes deep, where shadows twist and coil,
The murmur of the deep began to rise,
In watery depths, the soil of evil toil,
A lair of malice, veiled in mournful cries.
The moon, a witness to his fated quest,
Reflected courage in his steadfast gaze,

While Grendel stirred, an ancient force unblessed,
To snuff the flame of hope, to twist the praise.
Yet destiny would weave a thread most bold,
As steel met flesh in primal clash of might,
With every blow, the ancient saga told,
The sound of fate rang out through endless night.
In Grendel's eyes, a glimpse of sorrow's depth,
A creature trapped between the dark and light,
For in the heart of every monster's heft,
Lies a tale of longing, lost from sight.

III

With roar and wrath, the night became a storm,
As Beowulf unleashed his fury, wild,
In grip of iron, sinew shaped the form,
A titan born from ages, fierce and styled.
The walls of Heorot trembled with the sound,
As battle raged, the air thick with despair,
And Grendel, feeling fate's fierce grip unbound,
Knew fear, that taste of death, hung in the air.
But in that clash, where heroes meet their bane,
Beowulf found a strength beyond mere might,
A bond of kinship forged through blood and pain,

A dance of destiny beneath the night.

With one last strike, the silence fell like stone,

Grendel's howl pierced the heavens, pure and raw,

And in that moment, courage stood alone,

A testament to fate's unyielding law.

IV

Yet in the wake of victory's bitter taste,

A silence lingered, heavy with the weight,

Of choices made, of lives that lay laid waste,

And echoes whispered tales of love and fate.

For every monster slain, a story lost,

In shadows deep, where light and darkness blend,

And Beowulf, a hero at such cost,

Knew wisdom's price, and where the paths may end.

In battles fought beneath the watchful stars,

We find our truths in struggle's harsh embrace,

For though we claim the world is ours from scars,

The heart knows well the monsters we must face.

And as he turned from glory's fleeting light,

A man, a king, forever shaped by night.

LIFE LESSONS

The story of Beowulf and Grendel is a cornerstone of Anglo-Saxon literature, showcasing themes of heroism, fate, and the struggle between good and evil. Beowulf's epic battle against the monstrous Grendel imparts several valuable life lessons that resonate with the human experience, providing insights into courage, the nature of true leadership, and the inevitability of fate.

One of the primary lessons from Beowulf's encounter with Grendel is the importance of courage in the face of adversity. Beowulf, a young warrior from Geatland, willingly confronts the fearsome Grendel, who has been terrorizing the kingdom of Heorot. His bravery in facing a formidable opponent teaches us that courage is not merely the absence of fear but the willingness to confront it head-on. In our lives, we often encounter challenges that seem daunting—whether personal, professional, or existential. Beowulf's determination to fight Grendel serves as a reminder that true heroism involves facing our fears, standing up for what is right, and protecting those who cannot protect themselves.

Another significant theme is the nature of true leadership. Beowulf exemplifies qualities that define an effective leader: strength, integrity, and a sense of responsibility. He does not seek glory for its own sake; rather, he is motivated by a desire to help others and restore peace. This lesson highlights that true leadership is not about personal gain or recognition but about serving the community and making sacrifices for the greater good. In our own lives, we can learn from Beowulf's example, understanding that effective leaders inspire trust and loyalty through their actions and commitment to others.

The narrative also addresses the concept of fate and its role in our lives. Beowulf recognizes that his battle with Grendel may be influenced by destiny, suggesting that while we can strive for success and heroism, some outcomes are ultimately beyond our control. This understanding encourages us to embrace the uncertainty of life and to act with honor and integrity, regardless of the potential consequences. Accepting the influence of fate can provide a sense of peace, allowing us to focus on the choices we can make in the present.

Additionally, the story explores the theme of sacrifice. Beowulf is aware that fighting Grendel involves significant personal risk. His willingness to place himself in danger for the safety of others illustrates the idea that true heroism often requires sacrifice. In our lives, we may face situations where we must prioritize the needs of others over our own comfort or safety. Recognizing the importance of selflessness and sacrifice can deepen our connections with others and enhance our sense of purpose.

Lastly, the battle between Beowulf and Grendel symbolizes the ongoing struggle between good and evil. This theme prompts us to consider our own moral choices and the impact they have on the world around us. It encourages us to strive for righteousness and integrity, understanding that our actions contribute to the larger narrative of humanity. The story reminds us that even in the face of darkness, the fight for goodness is worthwhile and necessary.

In summary, the tale of Beowulf and Grendel imparts essential lessons about courage, true leadership, fate, sacrifice, and the struggle between good and evil. By reflecting on these themes, we can navigate our own challenges with bravery and integrity, striving to embody the heroic qualities that Beowulf represents. Ultimately, the story encourages us to confront our fears, embrace our responsibilities, and act with honor, leaving a lasting legacy in our own lives and the lives of others.

"The Fisher King" – The Arthurian legend of a wounded king whose health is tied to the land, exploring themes of healing and decay.

This poem explores the legend of the Fisher King, a central figure in Arthurian mythology. The Fisher King is a wounded ruler whose physical ailment is intricately linked to the health of his land, which lies barren and desolate as a result of his suffering. The story delves into themes of healing, decay, and the quest for redemption. In his search for a cure, the Fisher King becomes a symbol of vulnerability and the interconnectedness of personal and environmental well-being. The legend highlights the journey of self-discovery and the transformative power of compassion, ultimately reflecting on the nature of sacrifice and restoration in both the individual and the community.

I

In twilight's hush, where shadows blend and sigh,

A kingdom sprawls beneath a weary sky,

Once vibrant lands, now choked in bitter clay,

Whispers of sorrow haunt the fading day.

Upon the throne of gold, a figure wanes,

The Fisher King, bound fast by unseen chains.

His gaze, a well of sorrow deep as night,

Reflects the barren fields, devoid of light.

His wounds, not borne of battle's cruel embrace,

But from the heart's decay, a lost grace.

For every wound he bears, the land does bleed,

In silent prayer for solace, hope, and seed.

Once rivers flowed with laughter, bright and bold,

Now stagnant pools hold secrets long untold.

Yet in this aching stillness, dreams still stir,

A quest for healing whispers like a blur.

II

The knights of Arthur's realm, with hearts so brave,

Set forth to seek the king, the land to save.

Through mist and fog, where ancient echoes dwell,

They journey forth, their hopes a fragile bell.

They cross the moors, where whispers dance like flame,

In search of wisdom, glory, and a name.

But lurking in the shadows, doubts entwine,

What if their courage falters, lost in time?

In distant woods, the voices of the past,

Speak of a quest that shadows hearts steadfast.

A grail of light, a symbol pure and bright,

Could heal the king, restore his land to right.

Yet shadows loom, where Grendel's kin reside,

In darkness, they await, their hunger wide.

For every hero's path is fraught with strife,

And in their quest for light, they risk their life.

III

Upon the sacred shore where waters weep,

The Fisher King awaits, his vigil deep.

A chalice gleams, adorned with mystic lore,

Yet only those with courage can explore.

As knights approach, the land begins to stir,

Awakened by the hope of those who were.

The waters rise, reflections twist and play,

Illusions dance, revealing truth's harsh sway.

With swords drawn bright, they face the lurking dread,

As Grendel's kin arise, their hunger fed.

But in the clash of steel and primal roar,

The heart of man must face what lies in store.

In every blow, the king's own pain reflects,

As fate entwines with honor, and respect.

In blood and sweat, the battle's tempest brews,

A tempest born of sorrow, strength, and views.

IV

At last, the dust of battle starts to fade,

The king, once wounded, now with courage laid.

The chalice raised, its light begins to flow,

A river of healing, soft and slow.

In unity, the land and king reclaim,

Their rightful bond, igniting passion's flame.

For healing springs from courage, love, and care,

In every heart, a kingdom waits to share.

So let the waters cleanse the weary soul,

And from the depths of sorrow, we are whole.

The Fisher King, with wisdom gained from pain,

Now understands the cycles of the grain.

In every wound, a story yet untold,

Of life and death, of dreams both brave and bold.

For in the dance of fate and mortal strife,

We find the threads that weave the tapestry of life.

LIFE LESSONS

The story of the Fisher King is a rich and symbolic legend within Arthurian mythology that conveys profound life lessons about healing, responsibility, and the interconnectedness of individual well-being and the health of the community. The Fisher King, often depicted as a wounded ruler, embodies themes of decay and renewal, illustrating how personal struggles can reflect broader societal issues.

One of the most significant lessons from the tale is the interconnectedness between the individual and the community. The Fisher King's physical suffering and impotence directly correlate with the desolation of his land. When the king is wounded, the realm suffers, highlighting the idea that a leader's well-being is tied to the health of their people and environment. This lesson encourages us to recognize our responsibilities not just to ourselves but to those around us. It reminds us that our actions can impact others, urging us to strive for collective well-being and harmony within our communities.

The theme of healing is central to the Fisher King's narrative. His journey toward recovery symbolizes the necessity of facing one's wounds, both physical and emotional. The quest for the Holy Grail, which represents divine healing and enlightenment, reinforces the importance of seeking out what can restore us. This lesson serves as a reminder that acknowledging our vulnerabilities is the first step toward healing. In our lives, it encourages us to confront our struggles rather than shy away from them, as true healing often comes from understanding and addressing our pain.

Additionally, the story emphasizes the concept of sacrifice and service. The Fisher King, in his role as a leader, must learn to accept help from others, including the knights who seek the Grail. This dynamic illustrates that vulnerability is not a weakness but a part of the human experience. It teaches us that seeking assistance and relying on others can be an act of strength and community. In our own lives, we may find it difficult to ask for help, but recognizing the value of interdependence can lead to stronger relationships and a greater sense of belonging.

Moreover, the Fisher King's tale conveys the inevitability of decay and renewal. The cycle of life includes periods of struggle and suffering, but it also holds the promise of regeneration. The land can only thrive again once the king is healed, emphasizing that growth often follows hardship. This lesson inspires us to accept the natural ebb and flow of life, understanding that challenges are often precursors to personal and collective transformation.

Finally, the quest for the Grail serves as a metaphor for the search for purpose and meaning. It reflects humanity's innate desire for fulfillment and connection with the divine. The journey towards the Grail is fraught with trials, echoing the struggles we face in pursuit of our own goals and aspirations. This encourages us to embark on our personal quests, remain steadfast in our efforts, and recognize that the journey itself can be as significant as the destination.

In summary, the story of the Fisher King imparts essential lessons about the interconnectedness of individual and community well-being, the importance of healing, the value of sacrifice, the inevitability of decay and renewal, and the search for purpose. By reflecting on these themes, we can navigate our own lives with greater awareness, compassion, and resilience, understanding that our journeys contribute to the greater tapestry of existence. Ultimately, the Fisher King's tale invites us to embrace our vulnerabilities, seek healing, and support one another in the quest for fulfillment and harmony.

"The Lady of the Lake" – The Arthurian figure who gifts King Arthur Excalibur, tied to themes of magic and power.

This poem explores the legend of the Lady of the Lake, a mystical figure in Arthurian mythology known for her connection to the magical sword Excalibur. She gifts this powerful weapon to King Arthur, symbolizing authority, strength, and the divine right to rule. The story intertwines themes of magic and power, as the lake itself represents a boundary between the mundane and the supernatural. The Lady's character embodies both nurturing and enigmatic qualities, reflecting the complexities of power and the responsibilities it entails. Through this narrative, the poem delves into the interplay between fate, destiny, and the impact of mystical forces on human affairs.

I

In mist-wreathed woods where shadows play,

By waters deep, in twilight's sway,

A maiden glides on silvered stream,

Her eyes aglow with ancient dream.

The earth lies still, its breath a sigh,

As whispered legends float and fly.

In twilight's grip, where fate entwines,

The Lady waits, where magic shines.

Excalibur, the sword of kings,

In her soft grasp, the power brings.

From Avalon's heart, where time holds fast,

She guards the past, the future cast.

In shimmering depths, her secrets dwell,

In every wave, a tale to tell.

The lake, a mirror of heaven's grace,

Reflects the dreams of a forgotten place.

Here, destiny brews in enchanted air,

The crownless king, unaware, unaware.

II

Once, in the halls of Camelot grand,

Stood Arthur, a king, with a heavy hand,

His kingdom thrummed with discord's cry,

While darkened omens filled the sky.

For shadows loomed, and envy stirred,

As whispers of betrayal softly purred.

Yet in his heart, a flicker remained,

A longing for peace, his spirit unchained.

He sought the sword, the light of the land,

To guide his path, to take a stand.

Through forests thick and mountains steep,

He journeyed forth, his promise to keep.

But in the depths of his troubled soul,

Lay a wound, a fracture that took its toll.

The land grew barren, the crops lay dry,

As echoes of sorrow filled the sky.

In dreams, he saw the lady fair,

Her voice a balm, his burdens to share.

With every step, through bramble and thorn,

He felt the weight of a king forlorn.

Yet hope was a flame that flickered bright,

A beacon of strength in the depths of night.

Through trials fierce and shadows cast,

He pressed on forward, his die was cast.

A vision rose from the misty veil,

The Lady awaited, her power to unveil.

III

At last, he stood by the lake's embrace,

The waters stirred, as if time slowed its pace.

From depths unknown, she surfaced, serene,

With grace divine, a shimmering queen.

"Arthur," she called, her voice like song,

"Your heart is heavy, your path is long.

But wield this sword, forged in the flame,

And rise anew, to reclaim your name."

With trembling hands, he grasped the hilt,

In that moment, his doubts were spilt.

The waters swirled, reflecting the fight,

As shadows danced in the fading light.

With a flash of steel, the air did sing,

As fate and fortune took to wing.

Excalibur, a gleam of hope,

Brought courage anew, the strength to cope.

In that instant, the land awakened,

Life surged forth, no longer forsaken.

Yet in the heart of this glorious gift,

Lay the truth of power—a potent rift.

For every boon bears a weight to bear,

And kings are bound by the choices they dare.

IV

Now Arthur reigns, his spirit restored,

Yet wisdom whispers, a gentle sword.

For power is fleeting, like morning dew,

And love, a bond that must hold true.

In the heart of the lake, where the lady reigns,

Lives the truth of the world—its joys and pains.

As seasons change, and time flows free,

Remember the lake, where destiny

Awaits the seeker, the noble heart,

In the dance of shadows, where worlds depart.

For magic and power, like water, may wane,

But love's quiet strength shall ever remain.

So raise your sword, but keep your soul,

For in the end, it is love that makes us whole.

LIFE LESSONS

The story of the Lady of the Lake is a captivating tale within Arthurian legend that conveys important life lessons about power, responsibility, and the balance between magic and morality. As the mystical figure who presents King Arthur with Excalibur, the Lady of the Lake embodies themes that resonate deeply with human experiences and the complexities of leadership.

One of the central lessons from the tale is the significance of responsibility that comes with power. When the Lady of the Lake bestows Excalibur upon Arthur, she entrusts him with a powerful symbol of leadership. This act highlights that with great power comes the obligation to use it wisely and justly. Arthur's journey as king is marked by decisions that affect the lives of his people. This lesson reminds us that authority is not merely a privilege but a duty to serve others. In our own lives, we must consider how our actions impact those around us, understanding that true leadership requires ethical decision-making and a commitment to the greater good.

Another key theme is the relationship between magic and morality. The Lady of the Lake represents the magical forces that govern the realm, yet her gifts come with expectations. Excalibur is not just a weapon; it symbolizes the ideals of justice and honor. This duality serves as a reminder that power can be both a tool for good and a source of corruption. We learn that while ambition and drive can lead to success, they must be tempered with moral integrity. This balance is crucial in navigating the challenges of life, urging us to wield our own "weapons" — be they skills, talents, or influence — with care and conscience.

The story also emphasizes the idea of legacy. The Lady of the Lake's role in Arthur's rise to power highlights the importance of mentorship and guidance. Her intervention shapes Arthur's destiny, illustrating how the support and wisdom of others can significantly influence our paths. This encourages us to recognize and appreciate the mentors in our lives, as well as the potential we have to guide and inspire others in return. Understanding the impact of these relationships can help us cultivate a sense of community and shared purpose.

Moreover, the Lady of the Lake represents the mysterious nature of fate. Her appearance at a pivotal moment in Arthur's life suggests that destiny often intertwines with human choices. While Arthur is a central figure in shaping his kingdom, the magic of the Lady serves as a reminder that certain elements of our journeys are beyond our control. This lesson encourages us to embrace uncertainty and recognize that while we can strive to shape our destinies, we must also remain open to the influences that life presents.

Lastly, the tale speaks to the importance of courage and sacrifice. Arthur's acceptance of Excalibur and his role as king require him to face formidable challenges and adversaries. This highlights the necessity of bravery in pursuing one's purpose, even in the face of fear and adversity. It teaches us that courage is not the absence of fear but the resolve to act despite it. In our lives, we may face moments that test our character and convictions, and embracing courage can lead us to fulfill our true potential.

In summary, the story of the Lady of the Lake imparts vital lessons about the responsibility of power, the interplay between magic and morality, the significance of mentorship, the acceptance of fate, and the courage required to pursue our destinies. By reflecting on these themes, we can navigate our own journeys with a greater understanding of the responsibilities we bear and the impact we can have on others. Ultimately, the Lady of the Lake invites us to consider how we wield our power and influence, encouraging us to strive for integrity and purpose in all that we do.

“Sir Gawain and the Green Knight” – A knight’s test of honor and bravery in Arthurian legend.

This poem explores the Arthurian tale of Sir Gawain and the Green Knight, focusing on a pivotal moment in medieval literature. Sir Gawain, a noble knight of King Arthur's Round Table, accepts a challenge from the mysterious Green Knight, who appears in Camelot, seeking a test of bravery and honor. Gawain beheads the Green Knight, only to be confronted with the shocking condition that the Knight will return the blow in a year and a day. The story unfolds as Gawain embarks on a quest to honor his word, facing trials that test his courage, integrity, and the very essence of knighthood, ultimately revealing deeper themes of honor, mortality, and human fallibility.

I

In Camelot’s embrace where legends rise,

Amidst the stone and song of ancient skies,

The Round Table’s light, a beacon bright,

Draws knights of valor, honor in their sight.

Yet whispers ride on winds of fateful night,

A shadow cloaked in emerald, dread and might.

The Green Knight, borne of earth’s untamed grace,

Steps forth to test the heart of Arthur’s race.

Beneath the boughs where moss and ivy twine,

A challenge stirs, where fate and courage align.

"Who among you dares to meet my gaze?
With one swift strike, let valor blaze."
A hush envelops all, breaths held in fear,
For honor's cost, they ponder, sharp and clear.
Yet Gawain, young and bold, steps from the throng,
His spirit fierce, his heart a warrior's song.

II

The axe gleams silver under watchful stars,
A promise sealed, the price of honor bears scars.
One year to wait, then meet by the green tree,
Where courage will clash with fate's decree.
Through forests deep, he rides, the path unclear,
Each heartbeat echoes doubts, his growing fear.
A lady waits, with eyes like twilight's glow,
Her whispers weave like threads of fate's soft flow.
"Bravery, dear knight, is more than steel,
It's knowing when to bend, when to conceal."
Yet Gawain, steadfast, seeks to prove his worth,
A clash of ideals, a dance upon the earth.
In winter's chill, he finds a moment's peace,
Yet visions haunt him, doubts that never cease.
The Green Knight waits, a specter on the hill,

While Gawain wrestles shadows, seeking still.

III

The day arrives, the morn a tapestry spun,

Emerald hues awaken with the sun.

In the clearing, where fate and honor meet,

The air thick with tension, hearts skip a beat.

Steel against steel, the clash of wills resounds,

Gawain's resolve tested, where truth abounds.

With each swing of the blade, courage intertwines,

Yet within his heart, uncertainty defines.

The first strike lands, a shallow grace,

Yet in that moment, time slows its pace.

For honor's face is not just carved in stone,

It whispers of mercy, of battles not won alone.

As the Green Knight rises, a riddle unfurls,

"Do you know the heart, dear knight, that twirls?"

Gawain, trembling, sees beyond the fight,

The essence of honor, bathed in softer light.

IV

Upon the field, beneath the oak's wide shade,

A truth emerges, in the stillness laid.

Honor is not merely sword and shield,

But the courage to yield, the wisdom to wield.

Gawain returns, the journey etched in scars,

A tale woven in starlight, beneath distant stars.

In every heart, a knight rides through the night,

With lessons of courage, shining ever bright.

For life's true quest lies not in glory's chase,

But in finding one's self, in the soft embrace

Of humility's grace, of love's guiding hand,

In the dance of honor, where we all must stand.

So let the tale of Gawain and the Green Knight

Resound through the ages, a beacon of light.

In the heart of each knight, in each soul's refrain,

Lies the power of honor, in joy and in pain.

LIFE LESSONS

The tale of "Sir Gawain and the Green Knight" is a profound exploration of honor, bravery, and the complexities of human nature within the framework of Arthurian legend. Gawain, a knight of the Round Table, accepts a challenge from the enigmatic Green Knight, setting off a journey that teaches several vital life lessons.

One of the primary lessons from Gawain's journey is the importance of integrity and honor. Gawain's acceptance of the Green Knight's challenge reflects his commitment to uphold the values of knighthood, demonstrating that true honor requires not only bravery in battle but also a steadfast adherence to one's word. This lesson resonates with the idea that integrity is paramount in personal and professional life; when we make commitments, we must strive to follow through, even when faced with difficult circumstances.

Another significant theme is the concept of humility and self-awareness. Throughout the story, Gawain learns that even the most noble individuals can falter. When he ultimately hesitates to face the Green Knight, driven by fear for his life, he recognizes his own vulnerabilities. This moment of self-realization teaches us that humility is crucial; acknowledging our limitations and mistakes is a strength, not a weakness. It encourages us to embrace our humanity, understanding that we are all flawed and capable of growth.

The story also highlights the tension between courage and fear. Gawain's journey is a testament to the duality of bravery. While he initially presents himself as a paragon of valor, the threat of death forces him to confront his own fears. This teaches us that courage is not the absence of fear but the ability to act in spite of it. In our lives, we may encounter situations that challenge us, and it is in these moments that our true character is revealed.

Moreover, the tale underscores the importance of consequences and accountability. Gawain's actions lead to a reckoning when he meets the Green Knight for their final confrontation. The knight's revelation of Gawain's flaw—his failure to fully embrace his fate—serves as a reminder that our choices carry weight, and we must be prepared to accept the outcomes. This lesson encourages us to be mindful of our decisions, recognizing that they shape not only our lives but also the lives of those around us.

Additionally, the theme of nature and the cycles of life plays a critical role in Gawain's quest. The Green Knight, deeply connected to the natural world, represents the inevitability of change and the passage of time. Gawain's journey reflects the human experience of grappling with the forces of nature and fate. This aspect teaches us to accept the cycles of life—birth, growth, decay, and renewal—and to find meaning in our experiences, both joyous and challenging.

Finally, the narrative explores the concept of the ideal versus reality. Gawain's quest to prove himself as the perfect knight is complicated by his experiences, revealing that perfection is an unattainable ideal. This lesson encourages us to embrace our imperfections and strive for growth rather than perfection. It suggests that the pursuit of authenticity is more valuable than adhering to an unrealistic standard.

In summary, "Sir Gawain and the Green Knight" imparts essential lessons about integrity, humility, courage, accountability, the natural cycles of life, and the pursuit of authenticity. By reflecting on these themes, we can navigate our own lives with greater awareness and resilience, striving to uphold our values while accepting our humanity. Ultimately, Gawain's journey serves as a powerful reminder that the path to honor is fraught with challenges, yet it is through these trials that we truly discover who we are.

“Merlin and the Dragon” – The story of Merlin’s prophecies and connection to dragons in Arthurian lore.

This poem explores the legendary figure of Merlin, the wise wizard from Arthurian lore, and his connection to dragons as symbols of power and prophecy. Set in the mystical landscapes of Camelot, the narrative unfolds as Merlin senses an impending danger—a dragon that embodies both chaos and potential. The poem details his journey to unite the kingdom against fear and ambition, emphasizing themes of love, courage, and destiny. In a climactic confrontation, Merlin advocates for embracing the dragon’s fire, symbolizing the transformative power of love over hatred. Ultimately, the poem reflects on how unity and wisdom can overcome darkness, ensuring that both human and mythical legacies endure.

I

In mist-shrouded glades where ancient shadows dwell,

Where whispers of fate weave through twilight’s veil,

A wizard wanders, seeking truths to tell,

His thoughts entwined with time’s unyielding trail.

Here, among the yews, where memories entwine,

A tapestry of power, peril, and grace,

Merlin, sage of old, seeks wisdom divine,

In prophecies that pulse within the heart's embrace.

Born of the tempest, where fire and ice converge,

His spirit resonates with echoes of the past,

A guardian of realms where lost visions surge,

Where dragons stir beneath the twilight cast.

Each flicker of flame, a tale yet to unfold,

Each rustle of leaves, a song of fate's decree,

He bears the weight of destinies untold,

In every heartbeat, a shadow calls to be.

II

The realm of Camelot, bright with honor's gleam,

Yet lurking beneath, ambition's serpent coils,

A dragon stirs, its fire a looming dream,

A harbinger of fate where darkness spoils.

Merlin senses tremors in the waking ground,

A pulse of danger thrums in the air he breathes,

For kings may rise, but tyranny knows no bound,

And in the dark, betrayal silently weaves.

With wisdom as his shield, he journeys afar,

Through valleys deep and mountains kissed by snow,

To seek the truth that shimmers like a star,

In ancient runes, the fire's dance does show.

"Awake, my kin!" he cries, to those who dare,

"For love, not fear, must reign within our hearts,

The dragon's flame can purge the world's despair,
But only if we choose to play our parts."
Yet envy brews within the hearts of men,
For they fear what they cannot comprehend,
Their whispers coil like smoke, dark as a pen,
To seize the power that fate will not lend.
Merlin stands resolute, a beacon in the storm,
His heart entwined with truths both bold and rare,
For dragons, too, have spirits fierce and warm,
And only through love can they lay bare.

III

Then came the night when stars aligned with fate,
A gathering of souls upon the hill,
Merlin stood firm, the air thick with weight,
As thunder rolled, the world itself stood still.
The dragon soared, its wings a shadow vast,
With eyes like burning coals, it pierced the night,
"Behold," it roared, "the legacies amassed,
For only love can guide the heart's true flight."
With fire in his heart, he faced the throng,
Their weapons drawn, their eyes like ice and stone,
"Fear not the dragon," he called, bold and strong,

"For love shall conquer hate; you are not alone."

The skies erupted, lightning danced like gold,

As fire met steel, and courage filled the air,

Merlin's voice rang true, a prophecy foretold,

"Embrace the flame; let hearts ignite with care!"

The dragon's breath ignited passion's blaze,

Its fire a storm, a cleansing, raging tide,

As darkness fled, the hearts of men ablaze,

In unity, they found the strength to bide.

From ashes rose the hope of what could be,

For love, not power, held the truest claim,

The dragon's heart, entwined with destiny,

A legacy of light, a sacred flame.

IV

So now, dear friend, let legends weave their tale,

Of Merlin's wisdom and the dragon's flight,

In hearts united, let the dream prevail,

For love is stronger than the deepest night.

In every whisper of the ancient trees,

In every shadow cast upon the land,

The story lingers, carried on the breeze,

A bond of magic, forged by fate's own hand.

Embrace the truth within the tale retold,

For every dragon has its rightful place,

And wisdom shines like silver, bright and bold,

In the dance of time, the struggle, and the grace.

Remember, in the realms of night and day,

That courage blooms where love ignites the spark,

In every heart, the dragon finds its way,

And Merlin's prophecies will light the dark.

LIFE LESSONS

The story of Merlin and the Dragon is a compelling narrative within Arthurian lore that imparts profound life lessons about foresight, the nature of power, and the significance of understanding one's destiny. As a legendary figure and advisor to King Arthur, Merlin's connection to dragons and his prophetic abilities offer rich insights into the human experience.

One of the primary lessons from this tale is the importance of foresight and wisdom. Merlin's prophecies serve as a guiding light for Arthur and his kingdom, emphasizing the value of looking beyond the present moment. This teaches us that understanding potential outcomes and preparing for the future can help us make more informed decisions. In our own lives, cultivating foresight allows us to navigate challenges effectively, anticipate consequences, and seize opportunities that might otherwise go unnoticed.

Additionally, the story illustrates the dual nature of power and responsibility. Dragons, often symbols of strength and danger, embody the potent forces of nature and the unpredictability of power. Merlin's relationship with dragons highlights the idea that with great power comes significant responsibility. Leaders must be mindful of how their choices affect others, recognizing that power can be both a gift and a burden. This lesson encourages us to approach our own sources of power—be it personal influence, knowledge, or authority—with care and ethical consideration.

The tale also emphasizes the concept of self-discovery and identity. Merlin's journey involves a deep connection to his own nature and purpose. As he navigates the complexities of prophecy and magic, he learns about his role in the larger tapestry of fate. This aspect encourages us to reflect on our own identities and the paths we choose, reminding us that understanding ourselves is crucial to fulfilling our potential. Embracing our unique gifts and recognizing how they contribute to the world can lead to a more meaningful existence.

Moreover, the story of Merlin and the Dragon addresses the idea of interconnectedness. Merlin's prophecies are not just isolated events but part of a larger narrative that involves the fate of the kingdom and its people. This interconnectedness illustrates that our actions can have far-reaching implications, encouraging us to act with consideration for the community and environment around us. It teaches us that we are part of a greater whole, and our decisions can influence the lives of others.

Finally, the tale highlights the importance of embracing change and uncertainty. Dragons, as creatures of transformation, symbolize the inevitability of change in life. Merlin's prophecies often reveal truths that challenge the status quo, demonstrating that embracing change is essential for growth and evolution. This lesson is especially relevant in a world where circumstances are constantly shifting; accepting and adapting to change can lead to personal development and resilience.

In summary, the story of Merlin and the Dragon imparts valuable lessons about foresight, the nature of power, self-discovery, interconnectedness, and the importance of embracing change. By reflecting on these themes, we can navigate our lives with greater awareness, making choices that honor our responsibilities while remaining attuned to the larger narratives at play. Ultimately, Merlin's wisdom serves as a reminder that understanding our role in the world, and the forces that shape it, is essential for living a purposeful and impactful life.

“The Legend of Atlantis” – The tale of a lost, advanced civilization, exploring hubris, utopia, and disaster.

The poem "The Legend of Atlantis" narrates the rise and fall of the mythical civilization of Atlantis, exploring themes of hubris, ambition, and the pursuit of true wisdom. It begins by depicting Atlantis as a utopian society, rich in beauty and knowledge. However, as the citizens become consumed by pride and greed, they neglect the core values of love and humility. The climax reveals the catastrophic consequences of their actions, as a powerful storm leads to the city's destruction. Ultimately, the poem serves as a reflection on the importance of balance, kindness, and self-awareness, suggesting that true fulfillment lies not in ambition, but in love and connection.

I

In twilight's grasp, where shadows twine,

Beneath the depths of time's embrace,

There lay a realm, lost to the divine,

A dream, a whisper, a forgotten space.

Atlantis, draped in azure glow,

With towers kissed by dawn's first light,

Where wisdom's currents ebbed and flowed,

In harmony's song, bold and bright.

The ocean's breath, a guardian's grace,

Held secrets deep in its sapphire chest,

A sanctuary where truth found place,

And souls entwined in love's behest.

With artisans skilled, they carved their fate,

Spinning tales, their spirits soared,

Yet in ambition's relentless weight,

A longing stirred for power adored.

In lush gardens where laughter bloomed,

They sculpted wonders, each heart alight,

Yet shadows loomed where pride consumed,

As glory whispered, "Claim your right."

But time, like tides, will ebb and swell,

And even light can cast a shade,

In pursuit of dreams, the truth fell,

As pride unfurled its fatal braid.

II

A council met by the silver sea,

To ponder realms of might and grace,

"Let us forge a world where all shall be,

Where every heart and mind finds place."

Yet whispers turned to shouts of greed,

And in their hearts, ambition swelled,

With every stone, they lost the creed,

That love, not power, must be upheld.

With each grand structure, a pact was wrought,

A tower high, a vault of gold,

Yet cracks appeared in their paradise sought,

And darkness whispered, "You are bold."

A prophecy spun on fate's cruel winds,

Spoke of a reckoning to unfold,

Yet none would heed the signs, the sins,

As pride danced on, and truth grew cold.

Amidst the revelry, a maiden stood,

Her visions clear, her heart a flame,

"Let us remember from whence we've stood,

For love alone can keep us sane."

Yet echoes of laughter drowned her cry,

The revelers swayed in a wine-soaked trance,

And in their folly, they let hope die,

To dance with shadows in a tragic dance.

In the depths of night, the sea did churn,

A tempest brewed with fury untamed,

As stars ignited, the world would learn,

Of ancient wrath, of dreams unclaimed.

The mountains roared, the heavens wept,

As Atlantis trembled, a doomed ballet,

And in their sorrow, their promise kept,

Dissolved like mist at the break of day.

III

The night erupted in chaos unleashed,

Waves towering high, a cataclysm cried,

"Remember us," the fallen beseeched,

As their dreams shattered, the sea's wrath sighed.

The towers crumbled, their lights dimmed low,

And echoes of laughter transformed to moans,

"Where is the love?" they whispered slow,

As darkness swallowed their sunlit thrones.

The skies wept fire, the oceans roared,

In wild confusion, their fates entwined,

Yet in that chaos, a lesson soared,

That love once lost is never blind.

The ground shook fierce, the heavens cried,

As Atlantis sank beneath the tide,

In sorrow's grasp, their hopes denied,

And silence fell where once they tried.

IV

In depths where shadows gently rest,

A legend lingers, a haunting refrain,

Of hubris bold, of dreams once blessed,

And whispers echo in memory's chain.

So when the sea reflects the skies,

Remember well this tale of yore,

For in your heart, true wisdom lies,

And love's embrace is worth so much more.

Let not ambition blind your sight,

But cherish kindness, let it thrive,

For in the end, it's love's true light

That nurtures hope and keeps dreams alive.

Thus, from the depths of ocean's tears,

The tale of Atlantis shines anew,

To seek the truth through countless years,

In love's embrace, our souls break through.

LIFE LESSONS

The legend of Atlantis, often depicted as a powerful and advanced civilization that ultimately fell into ruin, offers profound life lessons centered around themes of hubris, the pursuit of utopia, and the consequences of disaster. This tale serves as a cautionary reminder about the fragility of human endeavors and the importance of humility.

One of the most significant lessons from the story of Atlantis is the danger of hubris. The Atlanteans are often portrayed as a society that, in their quest for power and technological advancement, became overly confident in their superiority. This pride blinded them to their vulnerabilities and the ethical implications of their actions. The story teaches us that arrogance can lead to downfall, urging individuals and societies to remain grounded and aware of their limitations. It serves as a reminder that no civilization, no matter how advanced, is invulnerable to consequences born from overreach and disregard for balance.

Additionally, the legend explores the concept of a utopian society. Atlantis is often depicted as an ideal place, flourishing with wealth and innovation. However, the quest for a perfect society can be fraught with challenges. The story reminds us that the pursuit of utopia must be approached with caution, as the desire for perfection can lead to neglect of fundamental human values such as empathy, equity, and sustainability. This lesson encourages us to reflect on our own aspirations for improvement and to consider how we can build communities that prioritize well-being without losing sight of our shared humanity.

The tale of Atlantis also emphasizes the importance of environmental stewardship. The civilization's advanced technologies and resource exploitation ultimately contributed to its downfall, suggesting a disconnection from nature and a failure to respect the natural world. This aspect of the legend resonates with contemporary issues surrounding climate change and environmental degradation. It teaches us that a harmonious relationship with the environment is essential for long-term survival, urging us to adopt sustainable practices and consider the impact of our actions on the planet.

Furthermore, the story underscores the theme of disaster as a catalyst for change. The cataclysmic event that led to the fall of Atlantis serves as a powerful metaphor for the consequences of ignoring warnings and failing to adapt to changing circumstances. This lesson invites us to view setbacks and disasters not merely as failures but as opportunities for reflection and growth. Embracing resilience and learning from challenges can lead to transformation and renewal.

In summary, the legend of Atlantis imparts essential life lessons about the dangers of hubris, the complexities of striving for utopia, the necessity of environmental stewardship, and the potential for disaster to drive change. By engaging with these themes, we can cultivate a deeper awareness of our actions and their consequences, fostering a more mindful approach to our personal and collective journeys. Ultimately, the tale serves as a reminder that while the quest for advancement and perfection is noble, it must be pursued with humility, respect for nature, and a commitment to the well-being of future generations.

"Sisyphus and the Boulder" – The Greek myth of Sisyphus, doomed to eternally roll a boulder uphill, representing futility and perseverance.

The poem "Sisyphus and the Boulder" reimagines the Greek myth of Sisyphus, a king condemned by the gods to eternally roll a boulder uphill, only for it to roll back down each time he nears the summit. This cyclical punishment symbolizes futility and the human condition. As Sisyphus struggles against his fate, he embodies perseverance and resilience, ultimately finding meaning in his labor. The poem explores themes of hubris, despair, and the potential for inner strength, suggesting that even in seemingly pointless endeavors, one can discover purpose and joy in the journey itself. It invites readers to reflect on their own struggles and the possibility of triumph over adversity.

I

In shadowed realms where echoes weave,

Beneath the weight of fate's decree,

Stands Sisyphus, with heart entombed,

In chains of stone and agony.

Once crowned in light, with laughter's grace,

He dared the gods, he scorned the wise,

Yet hubris masked his inner face,

And pride unleashed his bitter prize.

A boulder fierce, a mountain steep,

A Sisyphean curse to bear,

To push against the void so deep,

And dance within the gods' cruel snare.

In valleys where the echoes groan,

Each rise, each fall, a tale of woe,

To bear the stone, to toil alone,

In shadows where lost dreams bestow.

What dreams lie buried 'neath that stone?

What hopes entwined in time's cruel fold?

For even gods, with hearts of bone,

Knew not the depths of his ascent bold.

II

Thus day by day, with gritted teeth,

He faced the sun, the storm, the dread,

Each step a dance, a painful wreath,

A struggle wrapped in tears unshed.

The boulder surged, a glimmering shade,

Reflecting light yet shrouded fear,

And with each push, despair displayed,

A moment's hope would disappear.

The mountain laughed, its crags aglow,

To mock the fire within his breast,

For every rise must meet the low,

The heights of pain, the depths of jest.

He gasped for breath, yet forged ahead,

His heart a drum of pounding fate,

With thoughts of all the paths he fled,

And visions blurred by heavy weight.

Yet as he climbed, a thought arose,

Is this his destined, darkened end?

To bear the stone, to feel the throes,

Of endless toil with none to mend?

But in that moment, truth unfurled,

A flicker deep within his core,

In every struggle, a spark revealed,

A strength reborn, a spirit sore.

III

Then came the day when all seemed lost,

The stone slipped forth, the chasm wide,

Yet from that fall, he counted cost,

And in that void, his heart defied.

For in the silence where shadows creep,

He glimpsed the path, a lighted way,

That though the boulder crushed so deep,

His spirit soared; he chose to stay.

With fierce resolve, he took a stand,

His hands did grip the jagged stone,

No longer bound by fate's cruel hand,

In struggle, he had found his own.

With every push, a wisdom gained,

With every slip, a strength reborn,

In failure's grasp, he was not chained,

But found his place in night's soft dawn.

And so he climbed, the mountain steep,

With joy entwined in every strife,

The boulder less a burden deep,

As meaning carved a path to life.

He laughed at pain, embraced the toil,

In every ascent, a dance with fate,

For through the sweat, the earth, the soil,

He found his power, strong and great.

IV

Now tell the tale where shadows blend,

Of Sisyphus, the wise and bold,

For in his struggle, we can tend

To roots of truth that must be told.

Though fate may twist and turn in glee,

And boulders weigh upon our backs,

In every rise, we too can see

The beauty found in nature's cracks.

So roll your stone, embrace the fight,

For in the journey, wisdom lies,

In every tear, in every night,

We find our strength; our spirits rise.

Thus, Sisyphus, with heart afire,

Stands not in vain beneath the sun,

For in his toil, he found desire,

And in the struggle, he has won.

LIFE LESSONS

The myth of Sisyphus tells the story of a man condemned to an eternal punishment: rolling a massive boulder up a hill, only for it to roll back down each time he nears the top. This tale, rich in symbolism, imparts several significant life lessons that resonate with the human experience, particularly regarding the nature of struggle, perseverance, and the search for meaning.

One of the central lessons from Sisyphus's plight is the concept of perseverance in the face of adversity. Sisyphus embodies resilience, continuing his labor despite the futility of his task. This teaches us that persistence is a vital trait, especially when confronting seemingly insurmountable challenges. In our lives, we often encounter obstacles that may feel overwhelming or pointless. Sisyphus reminds us that the act of striving, regardless of the outcome, holds intrinsic value. Embracing our efforts, even when success seems elusive, can foster growth and character development.

Moreover, the myth highlights the theme of finding meaning in our struggles. Many interpretations of Sisyphus suggest that his relentless labor can be seen as a metaphor for human existence itself. Life is filled with challenges, and while we may feel trapped in repetitive or unfulfilling tasks, it is possible to derive meaning from these experiences. The idea that Sisyphus can find a sense of purpose in his eternal struggle encourages us to reflect on our own lives. Even when faced with monotony or hardship, we can choose to focus on the journey rather than the destination, finding fulfillment in the process.

The tale also underscores the importance of acceptance. Sisyphus's fate is unchangeable; he cannot escape his punishment. In acknowledging his situation, he exemplifies a form of acceptance that allows him to continue his task with a sense of agency. This teaches us that acceptance does not equate to resignation; rather, it can be a powerful step toward inner peace. By accepting the things we cannot change, we can redirect our energy towards aspects of our lives that we can influence, ultimately leading to a more fulfilling existence.

Furthermore, the myth of Sisyphus emphasizes the value of determination. His unwavering commitment to his task, despite its apparent futility, serves as a reminder that our efforts matter. This determination can be applied to personal goals, relationships, and professional endeavors. The lesson here is to remain steadfast in our pursuits, even when the path is fraught with obstacles or when success seems distant. The act of continuing to push forward, much like Sisyphus with his boulder, is an embodiment of human spirit and tenacity.

The story of Sisyphus and the Boulder imparts vital lessons about perseverance, the search for meaning in our struggles, acceptance of our circumstances, and the importance of determination. By engaging with these themes, we can cultivate resilience and a deeper understanding of our own journeys. Ultimately, Sisyphus's eternal labor encourages us to embrace our challenges and find purpose in the act of striving, transforming what may seem futile into a testament to our human spirit.

"The Phoenix" – The myth of a bird that rises from its own ashes, symbolizing renewal and resurrection.

The poem "The Phoenix" explores the myth of the legendary bird that rises from its own ashes, symbolizing renewal, resurrection, and the cyclical nature of life. It begins by setting the stage in ancient lands, where the Phoenix is born from flames and ash, embodying both beauty and struggle. As the narrative unfolds, it reveals the bird's journey through trials and hubris, highlighting the inner conflicts of pride and despair. The climax emphasizes the transformative power of suffering, where the Phoenix learns to embrace its fate, ultimately rising anew. The concluding reflection underscores the message that from every ending comes a new beginning, inviting readers to find strength and hope in their own struggles.

I

In ancient lands where whispered shadows dwell,

A timeless tale unfolds through flame and ash,

Of a bird reborn, its voice a haunting bell,

In twilight's grasp, a world begins to clash.

Upon a pyre woven from dreams long spun,

It dances through embers, a radiant fire,

In the heart of the blaze, the cycle's begun,

A symphony of sorrow and desire.

The heavens hold their breath in dawn's embrace,

As gold spills forth from the cusp of night,

A creature ascends, in a moment's grace,

Defying the dark with its fervent light.

From ashes cold, the promise shall arise,

With wings unfurled against the azure vast,

The Phoenix soars, unbridled in the skies,

Transcending despair, its shadow now cast.

II

In the cradle of myths, its journey takes flight,

Born of the sun's kiss, a vision divine,

In sacred groves where ancient spirits ignite,

Its flame flickers bright, a celestial sign.

Through tempests and trials, it learns to endure,

Embracing the paradox of beauty in strife,

In silence profound, its spirit stands pure,

A dance with the fates, the essence of life.

Yet hubris once whispered in echoes of pride,

As the Phoenix ascended, it soared ever high,

In the throes of ambition, it floundered, then cried,

For the fire that fueled it concealed its own lie.

With ashes around it, in stillness it found

The whispers of wisdom that linger in pain,

In the quiet of night, its heartbeats resound,

In the void, it discovered the path to regain.

From the depths of despair, a flicker ignites,

A spark of existence, a glimmer of grace,

In the cycle of time, the spirit takes flight,

Transforming the ashes to a warm embrace.

III

Yet in those ashes, a pulse of the soul,

A heartbeat of hope, undying and bold,

From the depths of the void, new life makes it whole,

In the tapestry of fate, the Phoenix unfolds.

With a cry that transcends the fabric of night,

It rises from remnants, reborn in the flame,

The cosmos rejoices at its radiant flight,

As it soars through the heavens, shedding all shame.

No longer confined to the weight of despair,

It learns through its suffering the strength of the heart,

In the radiant blaze, all darkness laid bare,

Each feather a promise, each flight a fresh start.

With twilight's embrace and dawn's gentle breath,

It paints the horizon in colors profound,

For within the struggle lies beauty in death,

The tale of renewal forever renowned.

So with every cycle, it dances on high,

A symbol of hope in the vastness of night,

In the realm of the stars, it learns how to fly,

The Phoenix, a beacon, a flame ever bright.

IV

Let us remember this tale of the flame,

That life is a journey through loss and rebirth,

In the ashes of sorrow, we find our true name,

For through every ending, new paths find their worth.

In moments of darkness, when shadows grow long,

Let the spirit of Phoenix ignite in our hearts,

For the struggles we face are the notes of our song,

In the symphony of life, each ending imparts

A lesson in courage, a dance with the fire,

To rise from the ashes, to soar ever free,

With each trial endured, we kindle desire,

For within us all lies the strength to be.

May we embrace what the Phoenix has shown,

That from every ending, new beginnings will spring,

In the cycle of life, we are never alone,

For in every heart's whisper, the Phoenix shall sing.

LIFE LESSONS

The myth of the Phoenix, a magnificent bird that rises from its own ashes after being consumed by fire, conveys powerful life lessons centered around themes of renewal, resilience, and transformation. This timeless tale serves as a reminder of the cyclical nature of life and the potential for rebirth in the face of adversity.

One of the most significant lessons from the story of the Phoenix is the concept of renewal. The Phoenix embodies the idea that even after experiencing destruction or loss, it is possible to emerge stronger and more vibrant. This teaches us that endings can be the precursors to new beginnings. In our own lives, we often face situations that feel like the end of the road—whether it's a relationship, a career, or personal aspirations. The Phoenix encourages us to view these moments not as finalities, but as opportunities for growth and reinvention. Embracing change and recognizing that we can rise anew can lead to transformative experiences.

Additionally, the myth emphasizes the importance of resilience. The Phoenix's ability to endure the flames and emerge rejuvenated symbolizes the strength of the human spirit. Life can present numerous challenges, often feeling overwhelming or insurmountable. However, just as the Phoenix perseveres through its fiery trials, we too can cultivate resilience. This lesson inspires us to face difficulties head-on, understanding that struggles can ultimately lead to personal evolution. By developing resilience, we learn to adapt to life's inevitable challenges, emerging from them with newfound strength.

The Phoenix also symbolizes the idea of letting go. The process of burning away to be reborn illustrates the necessity of shedding old habits, beliefs, or situations that no longer serve us. This act of release can be daunting, as it often involves facing fears and discomfort. However, the Phoenix teaches us that to grow and transform, we must sometimes allow certain aspects of our lives to perish. Letting go paves the way for new opportunities and experiences to take root.

Furthermore, the myth highlights the theme of hope. The Phoenix's resurrection serves as a beacon of hope in dark times. It reassures us that even in moments of despair, there is the potential for renewal and rebirth. This is particularly relevant during challenging periods in our lives when we may feel trapped or defeated. The Phoenix encourages us to maintain hope, reminding us that change is possible and that brighter days can follow even the darkest nights.

In summary, the story of the Phoenix imparts vital lessons about renewal, resilience, letting go, and the power of hope. By reflecting on these themes, we can cultivate a mindset that embraces change and fosters personal growth. The myth serves as a poignant reminder that, like the Phoenix, we have the capacity to rise from our own ashes, transforming our struggles into opportunities for a renewed and vibrant existence. Ultimately, the legend inspires us to embrace the cycles of life, understanding that every ending can lead to a beautiful new beginning.

“The Myth of Medusa” – The story of the Gorgon Medusa, whose gaze could turn men to stone, symbolizing power and tragedy.

The poem "The Myth of Medusa" explores the tragic tale of Medusa, a once-beautiful maiden transformed into a Gorgon by Athena as punishment for her beauty and the jealousy it incited. Medusa possesses the power to turn those who gaze upon her into stone, symbolizing the duality of beauty and monstrosity. The narrative unfolds with the arrival of Perseus, a hero who seeks to confront her. However, as he confronts her, he realizes that her terrifying power stems from profound loneliness and sorrow. Ultimately, the poem reflects on themes of beauty, power, tragedy, and resilience, suggesting that even in darkness, there is a possibility for understanding and strength. Medusa's story becomes a metaphor for the complexities of identity and the human condition.

I

In twilight’s grasp, where shadows weave,

A maiden’s sorrow haunts the night,

Once draped in grace, now forced to grieve,

Medusa’s heart, a flickering light.

In sacred halls of Athena’s shrine,

Where beauty flourished, pure and bright,

Jealousy’s hand, a cruel design,

Brought forth the darkness, stole her sight.

Once kissed by sun, now shunned by fate,

Her hair a nest of serpents' dread,

Each whisper echoes tales of hate,

As longing wraps around her head.

Transformed from muse to monstrous guise,

She stands in silence, trapped in stone,

For every gaze, a life denies,

A queen of grief, forever alone.

II

In olive groves where shadows sigh,

The men, like moths, are drawn to flame,

With hearts of valor, bold they fly,

Unknowing of the cost of fame.

Yet when they meet her chilling stare,

Their dreams dissolve, their hopes undone,

Each glance a dagger, sharp and rare,

Turning flesh to marble, love to none.

Among the whispers, a hero brews,

Perseus, young, with courage wide,

Armed with a shield to pierce the ruse,

He seeks the monster, love denied.

Yet as he hunts, his heart grows cold,

For what is valor in the face of pain?

To sever ties, to claim the bold,

Is it a victory, or just disdain?

The cave, a womb of dreams and fears,

Where echoes linger, lost in time,

Each heartbeat marks the passage of years,

A haunting rhythm, a mournful rhyme.

Medusa waits, a tempest deep,

In every glance, the weight of fate,

For each brave heart that dares to creep,

Is met with sorrow, cold as slate.

III

Then dawn breaks bright, the moment nears,

With sword held high, the tension swells,

But as he strikes, the heart, it tears,

For truth emerges where silence dwells.

"Behold!" he cries, "Your reign must cease!"

Yet in that clash, a deeper grief,

For she, a prisoner, seeks release,

Not death, but solace, sweet relief.

A flash of steel, the world stands still,

Her gaze, a tempest, fierce and wild,

And in that instant, time does fill,

With echoes of a broken child.

As stone meets flesh, the power flows,

Her beauty haunts, a bittersweet,

In death, the pain of longing grows,

A haunting grace, both dark and sweet.

IV

Now legends twist through ages long,

Of Medusa's strength, both fierce and frail,

Her tale unfolds in whispered song,

A testament to love's cruel trail.

For every gaze that petrifies,

There lies a truth, a lesson steep,

That beauty's bond can mask the cries,

In every silence, love's roots creep.

So let her story teach us all,

That power wears a heavy crown,

In every rise, there's bound to fall,

And in our hearts, the weight of frown.

Yet from the ashes, spirits soar,

In every end, a chance to grow,

For Medusa lives, forevermore,

In the strength we find from pain and woe.

In every shadow, courage blooms,

In every heart, a tale retold,

For Medusa's spirit, fierce, entombed,

Whispers of resilience, brave and bold.

LIFE LESSONS

The myth of Medusa, one of the three Gorgon sisters in Greek mythology, offers profound life lessons centered around themes of power, transformation, and the consequences of one's actions. Medusa's tragic tale, marked by her transformation from a beautiful maiden to a fearsome creature whose gaze turns men to stone, serves as a powerful metaphor for the complexities of human experience.

One significant lesson from Medusa's story is the exploration of power and its consequences. Initially, Medusa was a priestess in Athena's temple, renowned for her beauty. However, after being cursed by Athena for being violated by Poseidon, she became a Gorgon, embodying fear and destruction. This shift illustrates how power can be both a gift and a curse. It teaches us that power comes with responsibility and can lead to unintended consequences. In our own lives, we may encounter situations where our actions, even if well-intentioned, can lead to outcomes we did not foresee. Medusa's story serves as a reminder to be mindful of how we wield our influence and the potential impact on others.

Additionally, Medusa symbolizes the theme of transformation. Her metamorphosis into a monster reflects how trauma and suffering can alter our identity and the way we are perceived by the world. This transformation prompts us to consider how external circumstances can shape our lives and alter our self-image. Just as Medusa's beauty became a source of fear, our experiences can redefine who we are. The lesson here is to acknowledge the pain and struggles that may change us, while also recognizing the strength that can emerge from such transformations.

The myth also emphasizes the idea of perception. Medusa's gaze, which petrifies those who meet it, acts as a metaphor for how people can be judged based on their appearances or the first impressions they create. Society often tends to demonize individuals based on superficial traits or past actions without understanding their full story. Medusa, despite her fearsome reputation, represents the consequences of misunderstanding and the importance of looking beyond the surface. This teaches us to practice empathy and to be aware of our judgments of others.

Furthermore, Medusa's tale addresses the theme of victimization and empowerment. While she is often portrayed as a monster, it is crucial to recognize that her transformation was rooted in her victimization. This aspect of her story sheds light on the complexities of victimhood and the struggle to reclaim one's narrative. It invites us to consider how we view those who have suffered and to foster understanding rather than vilification. The lesson is about recognizing the power dynamics at play in our interactions and advocating for those who have been marginalized.

The myth of Medusa imparts valuable lessons about the nature of power, the complexity of transformation, the importance of perception, and the interplay of victimization and empowerment. By reflecting on these themes, we can cultivate a deeper understanding of our own lives and the lives of others. Medusa's story serves as a reminder that beneath the surface of fear and tragedy lies a tale of resilience and the quest for identity, urging us to approach our own struggles and those of others with compassion and empathy. Ultimately, her myth encourages us to embrace the complexities of our humanity and to recognize the transformative power of understanding and acceptance.

"Jason and the Golden Fleece" – The quest of Jason and the Argonauts, exploring themes of leadership, adventure, and betrayal.

The poem retells the myth of Jason and the Golden Fleece, exploring themes of ambition, love, and betrayal. Jason, the rightful heir to the throne of Iolcus, embarks on a perilous quest to retrieve the Golden Fleece, a symbol of kingship and power. He assembles a diverse crew of heroes, including the fierce Atalanta and the mighty Hercules, to navigate treacherous waters and face mythical challenges. Central to the tale is Medea, a sorceress who falls deeply in love with Jason and aids him with her magic. However, their love story is marred by betrayal and moral complexity, highlighting the tension between desire and consequence. Ultimately, the poem reflects on the cost of ambition and the fragility of trust in relationships.

I

In ancient lands where whispered legends breathe,

Beneath the watchful gaze of starlit skies,

A tale unfolds, where dreams and shadows seethe,

Of Jason, who would dare to claim the prize.

Scion of Aeson, noble, brave, and bold,

With heart ignited by ambition's fire,

He set his sail upon the seas of gold,

To seek the fleece, a treasure of desire.

The Golden Fleece, a glimmering mythic prize,

Rested high where ancient sorrows sleep,

Guarded by a dragon, fierce as death's own eyes,

A dream entwined with peril, dark and deep.

O Argo, vessel of fate's winding path,

With timbered heart, you carved the waves of chance,

Together bound to face the gods' fierce wrath,

A tapestry of glory, risk, and romance.

II

With heroes gathered, a bold, eclectic crew,

Orpheus, whose lyre could tame the wildest seas,

Hercules, the titan, whose strength we knew,

And Atalanta, swift as whispering breeze.

Their hearts ablaze, they faced the winds of fate,

Through siren songs that lured the soul to drown,

Past shores where shadows wove a web of hate,

To seek the fleece and claim the golden crown.

Yet trials loomed like storms on the horizon,

For in their midst, betrayal lurked, unseen,

Medea, sorceress of dark and dawn,

A heart entwined with love, yet torn between.

In her deep gaze, the tempest swirled and churned,

A yearning for escape from chains of night,

To leave her home, her past, and lessons learned,

And find in Jason's arms her guiding light.

But love, like ambition, walks a treacherous line,

For trust, once broken, twists like ivy's grip,

And dreams can falter when the stars align,

As choices made can lead to ruin's trip.

III

Through trials fierce, they reached the realm of gold,

Where Aietes, king, with wrathful glare did wait,

"Retrieve the fleece or face the flames, be bold,"

He roared, his eyes ablaze with ancient hate.

The dragon coiled, its scales like midnight's breath,

While Jason stood, his courage taut with fear,

With heart aflame, he faced the shadowed death,

To claim the prize, his destiny so near.

Yet at his side, sweet Medea, deft and wise,

Gave him the potion brewed from whispered lore,

To calm the beast with beauty's soft disguise,

Unlocking fate, where dreams and horrors soar.

And so, with heart alight and dagger drawn,

He struck the dragon down; its roar fell still,

The fleece revealed, a triumph after dawn,

A love entwined in strength, a tested will.
Yet as they fled, the skies began to darken,
For shadows loomed where trust had once resided,
A tempest brewing where desire hadarken,
A love now steeped in dread, and hope divided.

IV

As dawn broke o'er the shores of distant lands,
Jason bore the fleece, yet felt the weight,
For love betrayed now lay in tangled strands,
With trust eroded, bound to cruel fate.
Medea wept, her tears like silver rain,
For in her hands, she cradled bitter cost,
A love that bloomed from shadows, now in pain,
Yet hope still flickered, though their trust was lost.
Let the tale of Jason be a guide,
Of quests pursued with passion's fierce embrace,
Of love and loss, where shadows do abide,
And strength that falters in the heart's own race.
For though the fleece shone bright in glory's gleam,
It bore the weight of choices made too fast,
In every quest, remember love's true dream,
For in the end, it's love we dare not cast.

LIFE LESSONS

The story of Jason and the Golden Fleece is a rich tapestry of adventure that imparts important life lessons about leadership, courage, and the complexities of human relationships. Jason's quest, alongside the Argonauts, offers insights into the nature of ambition and the trials that come with pursuing one's goals.

One of the primary lessons from Jason's journey is the essence of leadership. Jason is not merely a seeker of the Golden Fleece; he is a leader tasked with guiding a diverse group of heroes. His ability to inspire loyalty and courage in others is crucial to their success. This teaches us that effective leadership is about more than just making decisions; it involves fostering a sense of unity and purpose among those we lead. In our own lives, whether in professional settings or personal relationships, the ability to connect with and motivate others is key to achieving common goals. A true leader listens, empathizes, and cultivates trust, much like Jason did with his crew.

Additionally, the tale underscores the importance of adventure and the pursuit of dreams. The journey to retrieve the Golden Fleece is fraught with challenges, but it is also filled with excitement and discovery. This serves as a reminder that the path to our aspirations is often as significant as the goals themselves. Embracing adventure encourages us to step out of our comfort zones, take risks, and learn from the experiences along the way. Jason's quest teaches us that while the destination may be important, the journey is where we grow, learn, and find meaning.

However, the story also delves into the theme of betrayal. Jason's eventual betrayal of Medea, who helps him secure the Fleece, highlights the darker side of human relationships. This aspect of the tale serves as a cautionary reminder that ambition can sometimes lead to ethical dilemmas. The betrayal underscores the importance of loyalty and the consequences of decisions made in the pursuit of personal gain. It prompts us to reflect on our own values and the potential costs of our ambitions. In seeking success, we must be wary of the impact our choices may have on those who support us.

Moreover, Jason's story emphasizes the significance of courage in the face of adversity. The challenges he and the Argonauts encounter—monstrous creatures, treacherous waters, and daunting tasks—test their resolve. This teaches us that bravery is not the absence of fear but the ability to confront it. Each obstacle they overcome strengthens their character and fortifies their bond. In our lives, we often face challenges that require us to summon courage and resilience. Jason's perseverance reminds us that overcoming adversity is a crucial part of achieving our dreams.

In summary, the story of Jason and the Golden Fleece offers profound lessons about leadership, the value of adventure, the nature of betrayal, and the importance of courage. By reflecting on these themes, we can better navigate our own journeys, learning to lead with integrity, embrace challenges, and maintain loyalty to those who support us. Jason's quest serves as a timeless reminder that the pursuit of our goals is often a complex interplay of ambition, relationships, and personal growth, urging us to seek not only success but also the wisdom to uphold our values along the way.

"The Legend of Gilgamesh" – A tale from ancient Mesopotamia about the hero Gilgamesh's quest for immortality and friendship.

This poem recounts the ancient Mesopotamian epic of Gilgamesh, a legendary king of Uruk who embarks on a profound journey in search of immortality and true friendship. Initially, Gilgamesh is a powerful yet lonely ruler, unsatisfied with his life despite his great strength. His fate intertwines with Enkidu, a wild man created by the gods to challenge him. Their bond deepens as they embark on heroic adventures, including defeating the monster Humbaba. However, tragedy strikes when Enkidu dies, prompting Gilgamesh to seek the secret of eternal life. His quest leads him to Utnapishtim, who reveals the futility of seeking immortality. Ultimately, Gilgamesh learns to embrace his mortality, finding meaning in love, friendship, and the legacy he leaves behind. The poem reflects themes of human experience, the nature of life and death, and the enduring power of connection.

I

In the cradle of ancient rivers, where time flows slow,

A city rises, proud and timeless—Uruk's walls aglow.

Gilgamesh, a king of might and grace,

Two-thirds divine, one-third a mortal's face.

In twilight shadows, destiny's whispers stir,

As gods and men weave tales of fate that blur.

Beneath the sun's unyielding, watchful gaze,

A restless heart wanders through life's endless maze.

The streets echo with songs of heroes long past,

Yet Gilgamesh, though strong, feels loneliness vast.

His laughter rings hollow, a chime in the mist,

For in every triumph, a deep longing persists.

What is power, if the heart's not intertwined?

What is glory, if true friendship is blind?

He dreams of a comrade, fierce and bold,

To challenge his spirit, to share in the gold.

II

From the wilds beyond, Enkidu, a beast, was born,

A man of the earth, where the sun greets the morn.

With hair of the wilderness, he roamed free,

Untamed by decree, he knew not the plea.

But fate's hand beckoned, as destinies align,

For Gilgamesh, in arrogance, sought to confine.

He called to the wild, to tame what's untamed,

To conquer the heart of nature, unashamed.

In the tavern of dreams, where visions collide,

They meet—two spirits, no longer to hide.

With strength forged in conflict, and laughter like wine,

Their bond blooms fierce, an alliance divine.

Together they venture to slay the great beast,
Humbaba, guardian, a terror unleashed.
In cedar forests, where shadows conspire,
They face the monster, igniting the fire.
With sword raised high in a dance of despair,
The air thick with courage, a potent affair.
They conquer the darkness, reclaiming the light,
But in victory's grasp lies the sting of the fight.
For gods, in their envy, watch with disdain,
Their laughter like thunder, a dark, looming bane.
Enkidu's laughter fades, replaced by a cry,
As the fates weave their tapestry—one must die.

III

In dreams, Gilgamesh sees a friend turned to dust,
A wild heart extinguished, as all things must.
He roams the earth, seeking the secret of life,
In mountains of despair, in valleys of strife.
Through scalding sands, where the sun's fire rages,
He seeks the immortal, beyond time's cages.
Utnapishtim, the sage, keeper of the flood,
Holds the key to existence, amid the ancient mud.
"Why chase shadows, brave king? What is life?"

The old man's eyes pierce through sorrow and strife.

"Immortality's lure is a perilous game,

For in forgetting, you'll find your true name."

Yet Gilgamesh, undaunted, pressed on through the night,

For the thirst for forever eclipsed all insight.

He faced the vast waters, a test of resolve,

To conquer the fear that shadows evolve.

"Cross the sea of death, if you wish to behold,

The truth of existence, the mysteries untold."

With each stroke of fate, as the waves crash and churn,

Gilgamesh wrestles with the lessons to learn.

In the depths of despair, he confronts his own fear,

A truth whispered softly, for those who will hear.

For in life's fleeting dance, and the beauty of breath,

Lies the essence of living, even amid death.

IV

Returning to Uruk, where the stars softly sigh,

Gilgamesh walks with shadows, his heart open wide.

For what is a kingdom, if empty and cold?

What is the glory, if no stories are told?

He gazes at the walls, with a newfound sight,

Each stone a reminder, each shadow a light.

In the fleeting embrace of a sun setting low,

He finds strength in the bonds that true friendship sow.

"Embrace your mortality, let it not bind,

For in love and in laughter, eternity you'll find."

He stands on the threshold, where shadows converge,

With the spirit of Enkidu, their destinies merge.

And as the stars twinkle, like memories bright,

He learns that in living, we conquer the night.

In the heart of the fleeting, true immortality lies,

In the stories we share, and the love that survives.

LIFE LESSONS

The Legend of Gilgamesh is one of the oldest known literary works, offering profound insights into the human experience through its exploration of friendship, the pursuit of immortality, and the acceptance of mortality. Gilgamesh, the powerful king of Uruk, embarks on a transformative journey that reveals important life lessons relevant to both ancient and contemporary audiences.

One of the central themes of the epic is the significance of friendship. The relationship between Gilgamesh and Enkidu is foundational to the narrative. Initially, Gilgamesh is portrayed as a tyrannical ruler, but his bond with Enkidu humanizes him, providing emotional depth and prompting personal growth. Their adventures together highlight the value of companionship and the impact of shared experiences. This teaches us that true friendship can inspire change, support us through challenges, and enrich our lives. In our own journeys, cultivating meaningful relationships can lead to self-discovery and a greater sense of purpose.

Additionally, the story delves into the pursuit of immortality. After the death of Enkidu, Gilgamesh is consumed by grief and embarks on a quest to discover the secret of eternal life. His journey, filled with encounters and trials, ultimately leads him to the realization that immortality is unattainable for mortals. This lesson encourages us to reflect on our own desires for legacy and permanence. Rather than seeking to escape death, Gilgamesh teaches us the importance of living fully in the present and making the most of our limited time. The quest for immortality is replaced by the understanding that a meaningful life is defined by our actions and relationships.

The epic also emphasizes the acceptance of mortality. As Gilgamesh confronts the inevitability of death, he learns that it is a fundamental aspect of existence. This acceptance is pivotal, as it shifts his perspective from one of fear to a focus on living a life of significance. Recognizing that life is finite can motivate us to appreciate each moment, pursue our passions, and forge connections with others. It serves as a reminder that while we may not achieve eternal life, our legacies can live on through the impact we have on those around us.

Moreover, Gilgamesh's journey reflects the importance of personal growth. Throughout the epic, he evolves from a self-centered ruler to a more compassionate leader. This transformation underscores the idea that growth often comes through hardship and introspection. The challenges he faces compel him to reflect on his actions and their consequences, fostering wisdom and humility. In our own lives, embracing challenges can lead to personal development and a deeper understanding of ourselves and others.

The Legend of Gilgamesh offers valuable life lessons about the power of friendship, the quest for immortality, the acceptance of mortality, and the importance of personal growth. By engaging with these themes, we can gain insight into our own lives, learning to cherish relationships, embrace the present, and face our fears with courage. Gilgamesh's journey reminds us that while life is ephemeral, the connections we forge and the legacies we create can resonate through time, enriching not only our lives but also the lives of those who follow.

"Anansi the Spider" – A West African folktale about the trickster god Anansi, who uses cleverness to outsmart others.

The poem narrates the tale of Anansi the Spider, a cunning trickster from West African folklore. Anansi seeks knowledge from the Sky God, who possesses all wisdom but challenges him to prove his worth. Gathering various animals—each embodying unique strengths—Anansi devises clever plans to outsmart the Sky God. Through wit and unity, he wins the challenge, demonstrating that knowledge comes not just from power but also from friendship and collaboration. Ultimately, Anansi learns that the true treasures of life lie in the bonds he forms and the stories he weaves, enriching his legacy as a storyteller and trickster.

I

In the cradle of time, where river and sky blend,

Beneath the vast heavens, where sunbeams conspire,

Anansi the spider, with threads that transcend,

Wove tales of the cosmos, igniting desire.

His laughter—a ripple in twilight's embrace,

A trickster of legends, both clever and frail.

He danced through the dusk, with an intricate grace,

Spinning the essence of joy, fear, and wail.

In the rustle of leaves, the night's tender sigh,

Elders gathered round, their wisdom a flame.

Anansi, the weaver, with truth in his eye,

Entwined mirth and folly, revealing life's game.

Through laughter and mischief, his spirit laid bare,

The paradox of existence, a dance in the air.

II

One fateful dawn, a challenge arose,

From the Sky God, whose dominion was vast.

"I guard all the wisdom the universe knows,

If you seek my knowledge, your worth must be cast."

With a glimmering eye, Anansi stepped near,

"I'll gather my kin; let us conquer this plight."

He called forth the creatures, each noble, each dear,

"Together we'll rise, let's emerge from the night!"

The lion, fierce-hearted; the eagle, so bold;

The tortoise, though slow, held stories of old.

In unity's strength, they plotted their fate,

Each creature a note in Anansi's grand state.

Through riddles and trials, they spun with the sun,

Yet Anansi's quick wits had only begun.

With laughter as armor, and cunning as sword,

He led them through mazes where shadows were stored.

III

At last, they arrived at the palace of clouds,

Where the Sky God awaited, his gaze a tempest.

"Can you outwit me?" he thundered in shrouds,

"Come forth, little spider, and prove your conquest."

Undaunted, Anansi wove a web rich with lies,

Each thread a reflection of power's cruel sway.

The first challenge unveiled, a question of pride,

Yet Anansi's laughter turned darkness to day.

With deftness and guile, he crafted in air,

A tapestry woven with truths laid so bare.

The creatures watched closely, their hearts pounding fast,

As Anansi, the spider, unveiled his grand cast.

With each twist of his web, he ensnared the skies,

Binding folly and wisdom in clever disguise.

In the end, with a flourish, he claimed victory bright,

For knowledge, though burdensome, was woven in light.

IV

Yet in his triumph, a truth took its form,

For power and cunning, though thrilling, can chain.

The whispers of friendship, the bonds that can warm,

Are treasures far richer than victories gained.

Anansi, reflecting, gazed down from his height,

In his web, he discerned the dance of the light.

In laughter and sorrow, he found wisdom anew,

That the heart of a trickster must cherish the true.

So he spun his stories, imbued with life's grace,

A tapestry woven with joy, dread, and space.

And children would gather, beneath the wide tree,

To hear Anansi's tales, both clever and free.

For in every trick, and each story well-spun,

Lies the magic of life and the bonds that we've won.

LIFE LESSONS

The story of Anansi the Spider is a celebrated West African folktale that encapsulates the qualities of wit, resourcefulness, and the moral complexities of cleverness. Anansi, often portrayed as a trickster god, uses his intelligence and cunning to navigate challenges and outsmart those around him, offering valuable life lessons relevant to both children and adults.

One significant lesson from Anansi's tales is the value of intelligence over brute strength. Anansi frequently faces powerful adversaries and daunting obstacles, yet he consistently relies on his cleverness to devise intricate plans that allow him to overcome seemingly insurmountable odds. This teaches us that while physical strength can be an asset, it is often our intellect and creativity that lead to true success. In our lives, we may encounter situations where quick thinking and innovative problem-solving can make all the difference, encouraging us to harness our unique skills rather than solely relying on traditional notions of strength.

Additionally, Anansi's stories emphasize the importance of adaptability. Throughout his adventures, Anansi faces various challenges that require him to think on his feet and adjust his tactics. This flexibility is crucial for navigating life's uncertainties. The lesson here is that the ability to adapt to changing circumstances and remain open to new ideas is essential for growth and success. In a world that is constantly evolving, being receptive to change can empower us to seize opportunities and overcome obstacles more effectively.

However, Anansi's cleverness also reveals the potential pitfalls of deceit. While he often outsmarts others for personal gain, his tricks can lead to unintended consequences, affecting both himself and those around him. This aspect of the tales serves as a cautionary reminder that while cleverness can be a powerful tool, it can also lead to ethical dilemmas. The moral complexities of Anansi's actions prompt us to consider the impact of our choices on others. It teaches us the importance of honesty and integrity, encouraging us to use our intelligence responsibly and for the greater good.

Furthermore, Anansi's adventures highlight the theme of community. Despite his individual cleverness, Anansi often interacts with other characters, illustrating the significance of relationships and cooperation. His stories remind us that while personal achievement is valuable, the support and collaboration of others can enhance our efforts. The lesson here is to appreciate the role of community in our lives and to seek connections that can help us navigate challenges together.

The tales of Anansi the Spider offer rich life lessons about the power of intelligence, the importance of adaptability, the moral complexities of deceit, and the value of community. By engaging with Anansi's clever exploits, we are encouraged to think critically, embrace change, and consider the consequences of our actions. Anansi's legacy as a trickster serves as a reminder that while wit and cunning can lead to success, true wisdom lies in using those qualities to foster understanding, cooperation, and positive change in our communities.

"The Legend of the White Buffalo Woman" – A Native American story of a divine woman who brings wisdom and peace to the Lakota people.

The poem "The Legend of the White Buffalo Woman" recounts the sacred story of a divine figure who appears to the Lakota people during a time of despair. She embodies wisdom and peace, bringing with her the sacred buffalo, a symbol of abundance and harmony. As she teaches the tribe about kindness and unity, they face a rival group intent on conflict. Through her guidance, they learn that true strength lies in compassion and shared humanity. The story emphasizes the importance of community, the healing power of love, and the enduring legacy of peace, symbolized by the white buffalo.

I

In the heart of vast plains, where the golden sun dips low,

Where whispers of the ancients weave through the evening's glow,

A tribe lingered in shadow, their spirits cloaked in grief,

Yearning for a vision, seeking solace, seeking relief.

Amidst the rolling hills, where sacred rivers twine,

A promise lay unspoken, an echo of the divine.

The Lakota gathered round, their faces drawn and pale,

With hearts like autumn leaves, caught in a mournful gale.

Beneath the twilight's blush, where stars began to bloom,

A figure graced the horizon, dispelling shadow's gloom.

Her skin, a silken canvas, shimmered like the moonlit sea,

Her hair, a flowing river, where dreams sought to be free.

Upon her back, a bundle, woven from the dawn's own thread,

A treasure trove of wisdom for the hungry soul to shed.

As she stepped upon the earth, the ground beneath her swayed,

For her presence bore a power that would not be delayed.

"Children of the boundless sky," her voice like crystal rang,

"For peace is but a whisper in the song of nature's clang.

I bring the sacred buffalo, a gift of life and grace,

A symbol of abundance, where harmony finds place."

And as she spoke these words, the darkness seemed to part,

Illumination flooded in, igniting every heart.

Thus, the tale commenced, beneath the canopy wide,

Of the White Buffalo Woman, who walked with strength and pride.

II

Once, the tribe despaired, their land barren and bare,

They wandered through the seasons, wrapped in a cloak of care.

Yet as dawn painted horizons with hues of amber bright,

The woman danced upon the plains, a spirit wrapped in light.

With each step she took, the grasses bowed in prayer,

The echoes of her laughter stirred the stillness of the air.

"Seek not the path of sorrow, nor let despair confine,
For in the heart of nature, the spirit's light will shine.
Let kindness be your arrow, let unity be your bow,
In the bonds of shared existence, the seeds of peace will grow."
The people, rapt in wonder, beheld her as she spoke,
As she shared the sacred teachings, a world from silence woke.
Through trials she would guide them, through storms of bitter strife,
Unraveling the wisdom that sustained their very life.
The sacred drumbeat echoed, a heartbeat shared by all,
Uniting souls in purpose, weaving bonds that would not fall.
Yet in the shadows' depth, a voice rose steeped in ire,
A rival tribe, embittered, sought to extinguish fire.
They came with arrows drawn, their hearts hardened like stone,
Oblivious to the truth that in their midst had grown.
But in the face of fury, the White Buffalo stood bold,
Her eyes aflame with courage, her spirit pure as gold.
"Bring forth your hearts of violence, let them clash against the sun,
For in the heat of conflict, the seeds of truth are spun.
Together we must forge a path, to bridge this rift of pain,
For only through communion can we learn to break the chain."
Her voice, a mighty tempest, stilled the air with grace,
And in that moment's silence, time revealed its face.

III

The clash of wills erupted, arrows soared through dusk,
Yet as the dust began to settle, hope replaced the husk.
"Look upon your brethren, see the tears that fill their eyes,
What glory is in victory when hearts are left to die?"
With every heartbeat echoing, she called for peace to rise,
Her spirit glimmered fiercely, a beacon in the skies.
The rival warriors faltered, their rage began to wane,
For in her gaze they witnessed the reflection of their pain.
"Are we not children of the earth, bound by blood and fate?
In unity lies strength, to heal the wounds of hate."
The air grew thick with tension, a moment held in breath,
As every soul remembered the balance between life and death.
In that breath of revelation, their weapons fell like rain,
The rivers of their sorrow washed away the chains of pain.
Together, side by side, they knelt upon the earth,
In the light of the White Buffalo, they found their shared rebirth.
They offered up their spirits, their fears dissolved like mist,
And in the warmth of love, the world was gently kissed.
Thus, the legend blossomed, a tale of hearts entwined,
A story spun from courage, a tapestry designed.
The buffalo roamed freely, a symbol born anew,

With every step they took, the land regained its hue.

From that day forth, the people learned to share,

To hold the hands of others, to show how much they care.

V

In the twilight's gentle grasp, as stars began to gleam,

The White Buffalo Woman smiled, a guardian of the dream.

"For peace is but a journey, a road we walk with grace,

In every whispered kindness, it blooms in time and space."

The elders wove their wisdom, the children danced in glee,

And in their hearts, the legacy of love would always be.

In the winds that touch the mountains, in rivers that flow wide,

The spirit of the White Buffalo walks forever by their side.

And in the stories shared around the fires' warm embrace,

Her teachings linger softly, an eternal, gentle grace.

For in the heart of every child, a spark of truth ignites,

To cherish one another through the darkest of the nights.

So let us hold this legend as we wander through our days,

To nurture one another in a thousand different ways.

For in the threads of kindness woven through our lives,

We find the peace of the buffalo, where every spirit thrives.

And as we share this journey, let love be our refrain,

A legacy of harmony in the dance of joy and pain.

LIFE LESSONS

The Legend of the White Buffalo Woman is a profound Native American tale that embodies themes of wisdom, peace, and the interconnectedness of life. This story, particularly significant to the Lakota people, imparts valuable life lessons that resonate deeply with the values of community, respect, and spiritual awareness.

One of the central lessons from the tale is the importance of spiritual connection. The White Buffalo Woman is not just a figure of beauty; she represents a divine presence that bridges the physical and spiritual realms. Her arrival brings teachings that emphasize the significance of maintaining a connection with the Creator and honoring the natural world. This aspect of the story reminds us that cultivating a spiritual relationship, whether through nature, rituals, or personal reflection, can foster inner peace and guidance in our lives.

Another critical lesson is the value of wisdom and knowledge. The White Buffalo Woman imparts essential teachings about how to live harmoniously within the community. She introduces sacred ceremonies, such as the pipe ceremony, which symbolizes unity and respect among the people. This underscores the idea that wisdom is not only about knowledge but also about understanding how to apply that knowledge for the benefit of others. In our own lives, seeking wisdom involves learning from experiences, respecting diverse perspectives, and sharing insights that promote collective well-being.

The story also emphasizes the necessity of peace and harmony. The White Buffalo Woman's arrival signals a time of reconciliation and balance for the Lakota people. Her teachings advocate for peaceful coexistence, compassion, and understanding among individuals. This lesson is particularly relevant in today's world, where conflicts and divisions often arise. Embracing peace as a guiding principle can lead to healthier relationships and stronger communities. It encourages us to approach conflicts with a desire for understanding rather than division.

Moreover, the tale highlights the theme of respect for nature. The White Buffalo Woman embodies the harmony that exists between humans and the natural world. Her teachings encourage the Lakota to live sustainably, respecting the land and its resources. This connection to nature serves as a reminder of our responsibility to protect the environment. By acknowledging the interdependence of all living beings, we can foster a sense of stewardship and responsibility toward the Earth.

Lastly, the story of the White Buffalo Woman is a powerful reminder of hope and renewal. The appearance of the white buffalo symbolizes transformation and the promise of a better future. It teaches us that even in times of hardship, there is always the potential for healing and new beginnings. This lesson encourages resilience and the belief that positive change is possible, no matter how dire the circumstances may seem.

In summary, The Legend of the White Buffalo Woman offers profound life lessons about spiritual connection, the pursuit of wisdom, the importance of peace, respect for nature, and the hope for renewal. Engaging with these teachings can inspire us to lead more intentional lives, foster deeper connections within our communities, and cultivate a greater appreciation for the world around us. The legacy of the White Buffalo Woman serves as a guiding light, reminding us of the values that can lead to harmony and fulfillment in our lives.

“The Trickster Raven” – A Native American myth of Raven, the trickster who brings light to the world, symbolizing cleverness and creation.

The poem "The Trickster Raven" explores the Native American myth of Raven, a clever and mischievous figure who brings light to a darkened world. Set in a primordial cosmos, the narrative follows Raven's quest to seize the sun from a guardian, illustrating themes of cleverness, community, and the balance between light and darkness. Through a playful challenge, Raven gathers other animals to join him in a dance of creation. Ultimately, he proves that light is meant to be shared, transforming both himself and the world around him. The story emphasizes the importance of unity, wisdom, and the joy of collaboration.

I

In the cradle of the cosmos, where shadows weave and sigh,

A world lay cloaked in silence, beneath a starlit sky.

The moon, a pale observer, shrouded in a silver veil,

While creatures wandered lost in dreams, through shadows thick and pale.

The earth, a vast expanse, where visions turned to dust,

Yearned for the breath of daylight, for warmth, for light, for trust.

In hidden realms of wonder, a figure stirred, a spark,

The clever Trickster Raven, whose laughter lit the dark.

With feathers dipped in mystery, and eyes like burning coals,

He flitted through the stillness, igniting dormant souls.
In quiet pockets of the night, he whispered to the stars,
"Awake, you slumbering spirits, and shatter cosmic bars!"
Thus, he soared through the silence, his heart a wild refrain,
Determined to unbind the dawn and cast away the pain.
For in his beady eyes, the universe would see,
The promise of creation, the birthright of the free.
So began the journey, where chaos met the wise,
The Trickster Raven plotted, beneath the watchful skies.

II

He sought the sacred waters, where first light kissed the night,
In shimmering pools of starlight, where echoes of delight
Resided in the ripples, like whispers on the breeze,
Secrets wrapped in twilight, beneath the ancient trees.
With cunning and with laughter, he spun a tale profound,
Of how to seize the sunlight and share it all around.
"Fear not the hidden shadows, for I am both the key,
And the lock that opens wonders, from dark to jubilee.
I'll trick the keeper of the light, I'll dance upon the air,
With every flap of raven wings, I'll chase away despair."
And so he flitted forward, through realms of dark and light,
His heart a drum of daring, his spirit pure and bright.

Yet lurking in the shadows, a guardian of the dawn

Held tight the sacred treasures, where light and life were drawn.

The old man with a staff, whose beard was spun from night,

Gazed upon the raven, his eyes like embers bright.

"Little bird of mischief, what folly brings you here?

To steal away the sunlight, to cast away the fear?"

The raven cocked his head, a glimmer in his eye,

"I come not to take, but to share the light from sky to sky!"

Yet words were but a riddle, a spark against the gloom,

The old man's laughter echoed, a thunderous boom.

III

"Then prove your heart's true courage, and let the games begin,

For light is not for taking; it must be earned within.

Dance with shadows, weave the night, create a path anew,

If you can outsmart the dark, the light shall dance with you."

And with a flap and flutter, the raven took to flight,

Challenging the ancient, to bring forth day from night.

Through realms of pure illusion, where dreams began to form,

He spiraled in a whirlwind, transforming chaos warm.

With cunning twists and turns, he played with fate's own thread,

Dancing through the currents, where hope and dread both tread.

He called upon the creatures, the whispering winds that blow,

"Join me in this game of wits, let's craft a tale to show!"
The fox with eyes of emerald, the wolf with spirit wild,
Joined in the grand ballet, like shadows meek and mild.
Together they spun laughter, like webs that caught the stars,
As they twirled in rhythm, breaking silence, mending scars.
The guardian, caught in wonder, could not help but gaze,
At the trickster's clever dance, the light that he would raise.
And with a final flourish, the raven drew the sun,
From depths of darkened waters, where all the light was spun.
He soared into the heavens, casting shadows far and wide,
The dawn burst forth in splendor, as light became his guide.

IV

"Now you've seen the folly of holding light too tight,
For it is not possession, but sharing that brings light.
The world awakens slowly, to colors rich and bold,
In unity and cleverness, we find the strength of old."
The old man smiled in wonder, his staff now dimmed and gray,
"Little trickster, you have shown the path to brighter day."
With wings spread wide in triumph, the raven danced on high,
For he had forged a legacy, a gift to earth and sky.
In the hearts of every creature, his spirit would reside,
The clever Trickster Raven, the symbol of the wide.

And in the tales retold, beneath the watchful stars,

The light became a melody, echoing from afar.

So let us share this wisdom, as we wander through our days,

In cleverness and kindness, we light the darkest ways.

For in the dance of shadows, where mischief finds its place,

We learn that creation blooms in every shared embrace.

The Trickster Raven whispers, in twilight's gentle call,

"Embrace the light within you, for it can guide us all."

LIFE LESSONS

The story of the Trickster Raven is a rich Native American myth that explores themes of cleverness, creation, and the duality of existence. Raven, often portrayed as a cunning and mischievous figure, plays a crucial role in bringing light to the world, which offers numerous life lessons that resonate deeply with both indigenous and contemporary audiences.

One of the primary lessons from the Trickster Raven story is the power of cleverness and ingenuity. Raven uses his wit to navigate challenges and outsmart those who would keep light from humanity. His cleverness serves as a reminder that intelligence and creativity can often be more effective than brute strength in solving problems. This lesson encourages us to embrace our unique skills and think outside the box when facing obstacles. In our own lives, leveraging our creativity can lead to innovative solutions and unexpected outcomes.

Additionally, the tale highlights the importance of adaptability. Throughout his adventures, Raven demonstrates a remarkable ability to adjust his plans and strategies in response to changing circumstances. This adaptability is essential in a world where situations can shift rapidly and unpredictably. Learning to be flexible and open-minded allows us to navigate challenges more effectively and seize opportunities that might otherwise pass us by.

The Trickster Raven also embodies the concept of balance. His dual nature—being both a creator and a trickster—reflects the complexities of life. While Raven brings light, he also creates chaos and confusion, illustrating that creation is often accompanied by disruption. This duality teaches us that life is not always black and white; it consists of both light and dark moments. Embracing this complexity can help us develop a deeper understanding of ourselves and the world around us, reminding us that challenges often coexist with opportunities.

Moreover, Raven's journey underscores the significance of community and connection. Although he often acts alone, his actions ultimately benefit the entire world. This illustrates that individual actions can have far-reaching impacts on the community. The lesson here is that our choices, even those made in the name of personal gain, can contribute to the greater good. It encourages us to consider how our actions affect others and to strive for a sense of interconnectedness in our relationships.

Finally, the myth of the Trickster Raven emphasizes the theme of transformation and renewal. Through his cleverness, Raven brings light to the world, symbolizing hope and new beginnings. This aspect of the story teaches us that transformation is possible, and that we can bring about positive change in our lives and communities. Even when faced with darkness, we have the potential to find light and inspire others to do the same.

The story of the Trickster Raven provides valuable life lessons about cleverness, adaptability, balance, community, and transformation. By engaging with these themes, we are encouraged to harness our creativity, remain flexible in the face of change, embrace the complexities of life, consider our impact on others, and seek opportunities for renewal. Raven's legacy as a trickster and creator serves as a reminder that while life can be unpredictable, our actions and choices can illuminate the path forward.

"The Journey of the Sun God Ra": – An Egyptian myth about Ra's nightly journey through the underworld and battle with chaos.

The poem "The Journey of the Sun God Ra" retells the ancient Egyptian myth of Ra, the sun god, who embarks on a nightly journey through the underworld. Each evening, Ra confronts the serpent of chaos, a symbol of darkness and destruction, as he seeks to bring light to the world. The poem explores Ra's inner struggles, emphasizing themes of balance between light and darkness. Through fierce battles and the invocation of ancestral spirits, Ra ultimately emerges victorious, illustrating the eternal cycle of creation and the importance of embracing both fear and hope in the journey of life.

I

In the realm where Nile's waters weave through sands of timeless lore,

Where whispers of the ancients rise and shadows dream once more,

A golden disk ascends the morn, igniting heaven's hue,

Ra, the sun god, blazes forth, his light a vibrant debut.

Crowned with serpent wisdom, he pierces twilight's gentle veil,

Each pulse of dawn awakens life, as shadows wane and pale.

Yet as day drifts into dusk, and twilight enfolds the land,

Ra ventures forth to face the night, chaos clutched in its hand.

Beneath the underworld's expanse, where silence cradles fate,

The serpent of destruction waits, its hunger insatiate.

A labyrinth of shadows coils, where doubt and terror twine,

Ra, the radiant warrior, steels his heart, his strength divine.

"O spirits lost in shadows deep, arise, your slumber cease,

For I am Ra, the blazing sun, I come to bring you peace!"

With every breath, he draws the light, igniting darkened halls,

A voyage steeped in peril, as night's cold curtain falls.

II

Through winding caverns, silence reigns, where lost souls softly weep,

Ra navigates the endless dark, where ancient secrets creep.

Each pulse of courage thrums within, as dread entwines his heart,

In shadowed corridors of time, he must now play his part.

"O ancients, rise from slumber; let your dreams be born anew!

For I am Ra, the fierce divine; I wield the light so true!"

Yet chaos stirs in corners deep, a tempest brewing fast,

A voice like thunder echoes, challenging the sun at last.

"Who dares disturb my kingdom vast, this realm of shadowed night?

I am the serpent of the void, the keeper of your fright!"

With eyes aflame like embers, Ra stands firm, a blazing shield,

In this clash of ancient powers, he summons strength revealed.

The battle rages fierce and wild, as brilliance meets the dark,

With every strike of sunlight, he ignites a sacred spark.

Yet chaos, cunning and relentless, coils tighter, full of wrath,
In swirling eddies of despair, they dance upon their path.
Ra's heart, a tempest of resolve, confronts the shadows' sting,
He knows each blow he strikes is born of light's enduring spring.
"From the depths of darkness, I rise; I embrace the ancient fear,
For without the night's soft whisper, the dawn would not appear."
In the crucible of struggle, he learns the worth of strife,
That the journey through the underworld illuminates all life.

III

With each resounding clash of will, the cosmos starts to shake,
Ra calls upon the spirits old, their strength no foe can break.
"Come forth, O ancestors revered; lend me your guiding light,
Together we shall vanquish this serpent's cursed blight."
The sky ignites with fury, as constellations weave and spin,
Echoes of the heavens rally, proclaiming victory within.
Stars become his stalwart shields, gleaming with steadfast intent,
While shadows tremble in fear, their darkened fate now bent.
The serpent hisses venom, its storm of darkness swells,
Yet Ra, with fervent brilliance, invokes the ancient spells.
"From darkness springs the dawn," he roars, with voice of flame and might,
"Embrace the light, O world; let the shadows take their flight!"
With this incantation fierce, the fabric of the void does bend,

As light breaks forth in torrents, the chaos meets its end.

In the heart of turmoil, the serpent's power wanes,

Ra seizes dawn's bright essence, dissolving all the chains.

In this cosmic crucible, he discovers deeper grace,

That even in the darkest night, light finds a sacred space.

For in the clash of darkness, the dance of life unfolds,

Each shadow is a whisper, each struggle, truth untold.

IV

As Ra ascends the horizon, his chariot blazing bright,

The world awakens gently, beneath a warm, embracing light.

Each creature stirs from slumber, as warmth spreads far and wide,

In the journey of the sun god, all chaos is defied.

"Fear not the darkened hours, for they too have their place,

In the eternal dance of life, find balance, find your grace."

With wisdom gained from battles fought, and shadows left behind,

Ra whispers to the wanderers, "Embrace both heart and mind."

For every journey taken, through darkness and through pain,

Holds the promise of the dawn, where hope and love remain.

In unity with chaos, the sun god claims his throne,

For light is born of struggle, in darkness, we have grown.

Let tales of Ra be shared, as dawn chases night away,

Of battles won through courage, and the dance of night and day.

In every heart, the echoes linger, of journeys forged and won,

In every soul, the knowing that darkness births the sun.

In the tapestry of existence, where light and shadow blend,

Ra's journey speaks of balance, a truth that will not end.

Embrace the night as teacher, the light as guiding spark,

For in the depths of struggle, we find our truest mark.

LIFE LESSONS

The story of the Journey of the Sun God Ra is a profound Egyptian myth that explores themes of resilience, renewal, and the eternal struggle between order and chaos. Ra, as the embodiment of the sun, represents light, life, and creation, while his nightly journey through the underworld symbolizes the challenges and darkness we all face in life. This myth imparts several important life lessons that resonate deeply across cultures.

One significant lesson is the importance of resilience in the face of adversity. Ra's nightly journey through the underworld is fraught with obstacles, as he battles the forces of chaos represented by the serpent Apep. Despite these challenges, Ra continues his journey, symbolizing the need for perseverance. This teaches us that life is filled with trials, but it is our ability to rise and confront these difficulties that defines our character. Embracing resilience can empower us to overcome obstacles and maintain hope even in the darkest times.

Another vital lesson from Ra's journey is the concept of renewal and rebirth. Each morning, as Ra rises from the underworld, he symbolizes a new beginning and the promise of light after darkness. This cycle of death and rebirth reflects the natural rhythms of life, emphasizing that endings can lead to new opportunities. In our own lives, we often encounter situations that may seem like an ending—a job loss, a failed relationship, or a personal setback—but these can also serve as gateways to new beginnings. Recognizing the potential for renewal can inspire us to embrace change rather than fear it.

The myth also highlights the significance of balance. Ra's battle against chaos signifies the ongoing struggle to maintain order in the universe. This theme teaches us that balance is essential in our lives, whether it pertains to work and leisure, personal ambitions and relationships, or individual desires and communal responsibilities. Striving for balance can lead to a more harmonious existence, enabling us to navigate life's complexities with grace.

Additionally, Ra's journey emphasizes the value of courage. Facing the challenges of the underworld requires immense bravery, reminding us that courage is not the absence of fear but the willingness to confront it. This lesson encourages us to confront our fears head-on, whether they be personal, professional, or emotional. Embracing courage can lead to personal growth and a deeper understanding of ourselves.

Finally, the story of Ra also speaks to the interconnectedness of life. As the sun god, Ra provides light and sustenance to all living things, illustrating the importance of nurturing our connections with others and the world around us. This lesson encourages us to appreciate our roles within our communities and recognize how our actions can have a ripple effect on those we share our lives with.

In summary, the Journey of the Sun God Ra offers valuable life lessons about resilience, renewal, balance, courage, and interconnectedness. Engaging with these themes can inspire us to persevere through challenges, embrace change as a pathway to growth, seek balance in our lives, confront our fears, and nurture our relationships. Ra's eternal journey serves as a powerful reminder that even in the darkest moments, light and hope can always emerge anew.

"Isis and Osiris" – The Egyptian myth of Isis's quest to bring her husband Osiris back to life, exploring themes of love, loss, and resurrection.

The poem "Isis and Osiris" retells the ancient Egyptian myth of Isis's quest to resurrect her husband, Osiris, after he is murdered by his envious brother, Set. As the goddess of magic and life, Isis embarks on a perilous journey through the underworld, facing trials and darkness in her pursuit of love. Despite Set's attempts to thwart her, Isis's unwavering devotion and powerful magic ultimately bring Osiris back to life. Their reunion symbolizes love's triumph over death and loss, emphasizing themes of resurrection, eternal love, and the enduring strength of the human spirit.

I

In the cradle of the Nile, where verdant whispers flow,

Beneath the sun's resplendent gaze, where timeless waters glow,

A tale unfurls of love entwined, where life meets ancient sand,

In echoing halls of memory, fate's weaving hand.

Osiris, lord of harvests, robed in golden light's embrace,

With Isis, keeper of the stars, her heart a boundless space.

Together they bestowed abundance, the earth their sacred stage,

Yet envy, like a serpent coiled, would soon unleash its rage.

Set, the dark and brooding brother, forged of spiteful dream,

In shadows thick with treachery, he plotted death's cruel scheme.

He crafted a splendid coffin, lured Osiris with deceit,

"Come, share my feast, dear brother, where joy and laughter meet."

But as the moonlight kissed the feast, betrayal took its toll,

Set cast him into darkness, sealing sorrow's gaping hole.

The river mourned, the stars grew dim, as grief engulfed the land,

For Isis, learning of his fate, stood silent, heart in hand.

With every step she took through night, her heart a heavy stone,

In search of her beloved, she felt the chill of being alone.

Through tombs of ancient whispers, her spirit would not break,

For love, a flame that flickers still, ignited her to wake.

She called upon the sacred ones, the guardians of the night,

Anubis with his solemn gaze, and Thoth, the scribe of light.

II

Through veils of night, she journeyed forth, a queen in sorrow's guise,

Her heart a vessel overflowing, where hope and anguish rise.

"Osiris, my beloved, through shadows deep I roam,

With every tear a promise made, I'll bring your spirit home."

The winds carried her whispers, entwined with ancient lore,

As she traversed the silent realms, her love an endless roar.

In every crypt she wandered, where phantoms held their sway,

Her magic sang in silent tones, a hymn to guide the way.

Yet Set, the envious tempest, cast darkness on her path,

With wrath and shadowed vengeance, he sought to stoke his wrath.

"Your love is but a fleeting flame; it cannot pierce the veil,

In my domain, all light shall fade; your heart shall surely pale."

But Isis, fierce with love's resolve, summoned forth her might,

With staff adorned in sacred gems, she dared to face the night.

"By the blood of earth and sky, I conjure light from fate,

For love is the eternal flame that shall not bend nor break."

The heavens trembled at her words, as thunder shook the air,

The battle raged in silence, a clash of love and despair.

III

In tempest's eye, she found her strength, a power born of grief,

As shadows danced in mocking jest, she sought the light's belief.

"Set, release my husband's soul; let love's sweet light unfold,

For I am the eternal spark, a truth that cannot fold."

Yet Set, cloaked in bitterness, laughed cruelly in reply,

"Your love is but a fleeting dream; beneath my reign, you die!"

But through the storm, Osiris stirred, a whisper on the breeze,

"Isis, my beloved, call forth the ancient keys."

With a final surge of magic, she shattered Set's cruel chain,

Her heart, a blazing furnace, turned sorrow into gain.

In a flash of radiant brilliance, Osiris rose anew,

A phoenix from the ashes, where hope once bid adieu.

Together they emerged, reborn, as dawn painted the skies,

For love had triumphed over death, and night had met its guise.

In the warmth of the sun's embrace, they danced on sacred ground,

A testament to love's fierce light, where miracles abound.

Isis and Osiris, intertwined, in the light they found their place,

In every heartbeat, every breath, their spirits interlace.

IV

In the tender light of morning, they stood against the dawn,

Isis, queen of magic, and Osiris, newly drawn.

"From darkness springs the life anew; from loss, the heart grows strong,

In every tear, a lesson learned; in every night, a song."

The Nile, a witness to their love, flowed freely as they twirled,

A testament to the power that transcends the mortal world.

In tales spun by the fireside, their legend lives and breathes,

Of love that crossed the boundaries where life and death weaves.

For in the arms of the divine, they found their sacred trust,

In love, there lies a power profound, eternal as the dust.

So let their story echo through the ages and the sands,

That love, once lost, may rise again, ignited by their hands.

Thus, Isis and Osiris teach of loss and resurrection,

Of love that binds beyond the grave, a divine connection.

In every heart that beats in time, their legacy will thrive,

For love, undying, seeks the light, and through it, we survive.

In darkness, find the flame anew; let shadows guide your way,

For love's embrace is everlasting, in every night and day.

LIFE LESSONS

The myth of Isis and Osiris is a powerful tale from ancient Egyptian mythology that explores profound themes of love, loss, and resurrection. This narrative not only captivates with its drama but also imparts several essential life lessons that resonate deeply with human experience.

One of the primary lessons from this myth is the power of love. Isis's unwavering devotion to her husband Osiris is a central theme. Despite the tragic circumstances surrounding his death, her determination to revive him demonstrates how love can inspire individuals to face seemingly insurmountable challenges. This serves as a reminder that love is a potent force, motivating us to take action and endure hardships for those we care about. It teaches us that genuine love can drive us to go beyond our limits in pursuit of what truly matters.

Another significant lesson is the importance of perseverance in the face of adversity. Isis encounters numerous obstacles in her quest to resurrect Osiris, including betrayal and the need to gather fragmented pieces of his body. Her relentless effort symbolizes the necessity of resilience and determination when confronted with difficulties. This teaches us that setbacks are a natural part of life, but it is our ability to persevere that ultimately leads to success and fulfillment.

The theme of loss and grief is also prominent in this story. Isis's mourning for Osiris highlights the pain of losing a loved one and the journey through grief. This aspect of the narrative reminds us that experiencing loss is a universal human condition. It encourages us to acknowledge our feelings, process our grief, and seek healing. The story illustrates that while loss can be overwhelming, it can also lead to personal growth and transformation.

Moreover, the myth emphasizes the concept of resurrection and renewal. Osiris's return to life symbolizes hope and the possibility of new beginnings after despair. This theme encourages us to view endings not merely as conclusions but as opportunities for rebirth and transformation. It suggests that, much like nature, we can emerge stronger from our trials and tribulations.

The myth of Isis and Osiris also teaches the value of community and support. Isis's efforts to gather help from other deities underscore the importance of relying on others during difficult times. This reminds us that seeking support from friends, family, or community can be vital in navigating life's challenges. It encourages us to build and maintain relationships that provide strength and comfort.

The story of Isis and Osiris offers profound life lessons about love, perseverance, grief, resurrection, and the importance of community. Engaging with these themes can inspire us to cultivate love in our lives, remain steadfast in the face of adversity, process our emotions, embrace new beginnings, and seek support from those around us. This myth serves as a timeless reminder of the resilience of the human spirit and the enduring power of love.

"The Legend of Romulus and Remus" – The Roman myth of the twin brothers raised by a she-wolf, who founded the city of Rome.

This poem explores the myth of Romulus and Remus, twin brothers in ancient Rome raised by a she-wolf after being abandoned. Destined for greatness, they grew into strong leaders but were torn apart by ambition and jealousy. As they sought to establish a new city, conflicts arose, culminating in a tragic confrontation. Romulus killed Remus in a fit of rage, marking the founding of Rome with bloodshed and betrayal. The tale reflects themes of love, loss, and the complexities of power, illustrating how ambition can fracture even the closest bonds, leaving a legacy of both greatness and sorrow.

I

In ancient lands where shadows twist and sigh,

Where Tiber winds through valleys lush and wide,

Two sons of Mars, beneath a sable sky,

Were cast adrift upon the world's dark tide.

Their cradle wrought from reeds, a woven fate,

A silent witness to a royal woe,

From womb of conflict, love and hate did sate

The flames of myth, as legends ebb and flow.

The she-wolf's heart, fierce guardian of the young,

Embraced the boys in warmth, fierce, wild, and free;

Upon her milk and might, their lives were strung,
In wilds where echoes sang of destiny.
With every howl beneath the argent moon,
They learned the language of the earth and air,
Their laughter danced like sunlit silver dune,
In untamed realms where dreams dispelled despair.
Yet in their veins, the pulse of warriors' pride,
Destined for greatness, bound to rise and roam,
A kingdom forged in strife, where dreams collide,
To claim the soil that would one day be Rome.
But shadowed hearts, entwined with fate's cruel thread,
Bore whispers of a future wrapped in night,
Where love would twist, where brother's bond would shred,
In search of power, passion turned to blight.

II

As time unfurled its wings of choice and chance,
The twins grew strong, like oaks from ancient seed,
Yet whispered winds bore tales of power's dance,
Of kingship's promise, and of bitter greed.
In visions dark, the gods their fates entwined,
While silent, watchful, fate in shadows wept,
For jealousy and love, so tightly twined,

Would seal the fate of brothers born to step.

Upon the sacred hills, the brothers stood,

Romulus, with fire blazing in his eyes,

While Remus laughed, dismissing brotherhood,

Yet dreams of power sparked the darkened skies.

In arguments that echoed through the night,

They spoke of cities forged on strength and might,

A struggle born of iron will and fight,

Where love once thrived, now darkness took to flight.

But ancient fears, like shadows, crept and loomed,

Their hearts a battleground, a restless shore,

For in the quiet corners, doom was groomed,

As loyalty was twisted by desire.

They gathered followers, a throng did swell,

While ancient stones bore witness to their plight,

As fate began to weave its fateful spell,

And stars above, like sentinels, took flight.

III

Upon the Palatine, the fateful day,

Romulus stood, a tempest in his gaze,

While Remus, with a smile, dismissed the fray,

Unknowing of the storm that would ablaze.

With swords drawn high, the brothers faced their kin,

A moment's pause—the world held breath in time—

Yet hatred's seed, once planted deep within,

Would bloom in blood, a bitter, cursed crime.

In fury's grasp, they clashed with all their might,

The heavens split as thunder rumbled low,

As siblings turned to foes in cruel twilight,

The ground beneath them trembled with their woe.

And in that clash of steel and shattered dreams,

The echoes of their laughter turned to cries,

The she-wolf wept, her heart torn at the seams,

As destiny unveiled its harsh disguise.

With one swift strike, Romulus stood alone,

While Remus fell beneath the weight of fate,

The city born from blood and bone was grown,

Yet love was lost, and peace would not await.

The walls of Rome rose high, adorned with strife,

As shadows cast by brothers stained the ground,

A legacy of loss, a tale of life,

In whispered winds, their names forever bound.

IV

Now wander, weary traveler, through this land,

Where ruins whisper of a time long past,

The twin-born tale, where love and blood did stand,

In echoes deep, their shadows hold us fast.

For in the rise of cities, in their fall,

Lies truth of bonds that love and power tear,

In every stone, a story to enthrall,

Of brothers lost, of burdens we all bear.

Thus Rome, a city steeped in myth and pain,

Stands testament to dreams that once took flight,

Yet from the ashes, hope can rise again,

A cycle of the dark embracing light.

For every ending holds a seed of birth,

In every loss, a lesson learned anew,

The tale of Romulus, of worth and worth,

Reminds us all of love's enduring view.

LIFE LESSONS

The legend of Romulus and Remus is a foundational myth of ancient Rome, encapsulating themes of survival, rivalry, and the complexities of leadership. This story not only recounts the dramatic tale of twin brothers raised by a she-wolf but also imparts several essential life lessons that remain relevant today.

One key lesson from the story is the importance of resilience and survival. Romulus and Remus, abandoned as infants, face extreme adversity yet manage to survive against all odds, thanks to the nurturing care of a she-wolf. Their survival illustrates the idea that with resilience and the right support, individuals can overcome even the most challenging circumstances. This resonates with the notion that difficult beginnings do not dictate future outcomes; rather, determination and adaptability can lead to success.

The myth also explores the theme of brotherhood and loyalty. Initially, Romulus and Remus share a strong bond, united in their quest for survival and their dream of establishing a city. However, their relationship becomes strained as they vie for power and recognition. This evolution reflects the complexities of human relationships, emphasizing that while bonds of loyalty can be strong, ambition and rivalry can complicate even the closest ties. The lesson here is that loyalty must be nurtured, and clear communication is vital to maintaining healthy relationships.

Another important theme is the idea of leadership and responsibility. Romulus ultimately becomes the founder of Rome after a violent conflict with Remus. This act of fratricide serves as a cautionary tale about the darker side of ambition and the heavy burden of leadership. It reminds us that with power comes responsibility, and the choices we make can have profound consequences not only for ourselves but for others as well. The story urges aspiring leaders to consider the ethical implications of their decisions and to strive for unity rather than division.

The legend of Romulus and Remus also touches upon the theme of identity and belonging. As they grow, the twins grapple with their origins and the legacy they wish to create. Their journey underscores the importance of understanding one's roots while also shaping one's own destiny. This encourages individuals to reflect on their backgrounds and how these experiences influence their identity and aspirations.

Finally, the myth highlights the theme of the founding of communities. The eventual establishment of Rome symbolizes the power of vision and collaboration. It shows that while individual achievements are important, the collective effort of a community can lead to greatness. This serves as a reminder of the importance of working together towards a common goal, fostering unity, and building supportive networks.

The legend of Romulus and Remus imparts valuable lessons about resilience, loyalty, leadership, identity, and the power of community. Engaging with these themes encourages us to reflect on our own relationships, ambitions, and responsibilities while reminding us of the strength that can be found in unity and collaboration. This myth remains a timeless reflection on the complexities of human experience and the enduring quest for belonging and purpose.

“The Chinese Dragon and the Pearl” – A tale about dragons as symbols of power and prosperity in Chinese mythology.

The poem "The Dragon and the Pearl" retells a Chinese myth where a powerful dragon guards a precious pearl, symbolizing prosperity and fortune. Two ambitious brothers, driven by greed, seek to possess the pearl, believing it will grant them ultimate power. However, their rivalry leads to tragedy when one brother falls, revealing the destructive nature of their desires. The dragon, embodying wisdom and strength, mourns the loss of potential and love, illustrating that true wealth lies not in material gain but in the bonds of kinship and understanding. Ultimately, the tale emphasizes the importance of love over ambition.

I

In ancient realms where mountains touch the skies,

Where rivers whisper tales of fate entwined,

A dragon coiled in mist, with emerald eyes,

Guarded a pearl, a gem both rare and blind.

Born of the ocean’s sigh and moonlit grace,

The pearl cradled secrets of fortune's glow,

A symbol of abundance, dreams interlaced,

In depths where chaos and tranquility flow.

Beneath the stars, the villages in awe,

Spoke of the dragon, fierce yet wise and old,

A sentinel of treasures, both feared and raw,

Yet shadows hinted at a heart grown cold.

For power corrupts the purest of desires,

And in the light, the dark can softly creep;

What once inspired now kindles ancient fires,

As innocence is cast into the deep.

II

Once, in a time when laughter graced the air,

Two brothers ventured forth, hearts intertwined,

With visions bright of glory, wealth laid bare,

They sought the pearl beneath the endless sky.

But fate, a weaver with a cunning hand,

Entwined their souls with threads of envy's thread,

For ambition's siren call can cloud the grand,

Leading noble hearts to paths where angels dread.

The dragon sensed the tempest brewing deep,

And summoned storms, the heavens roared in strife,

Yet the brothers pressed, as if bound by sleep,

Deaf to the love that thrummed within their life.

In caves adorned with shadows, whispers grew,

The brothers plotted, hearts consumed by spite,

To seize the pearl, believing power true,

Yet darkness waits where love is cast from light.

III

In twilight's clutch, the fateful clash unfurled,

The brothers faced the dragon's fierce embrace,

As thunder cracked, and nature's fury swirled,

They glimpsed not foes, but mirrors of their grace.

The dragon soared, a tempest fierce and bold,

Breath of fire met ambition's fleeting spark,

In that brief moment, wisdom's tale retold:

The pearl's true worth—illumination's arc.

Yet greed, a venom, stilled their reasoned plea,

With a single blow, the elder brother fell,

His dreams of power now scattered like debris,

In that lost moment, love became a shell.

The dragon's heart, now heavy with the weight,

Of squandered potential, wept for what had been,

A world once vibrant, now bound by fate,

The pearl lay still, a witness to the scene.

IV

With dawn's first blush, the dragon spread its wings,

In silence, felt the echoes of despair,

For power's lure is but a fleeting thing,

And love, the truest treasure, always rare.

The pearl, once sought for wealth, now gleamed with grace,

A promise held in gentle, patient hands,

In unity, the brothers lost their place,

Yet in the dragon's eyes, their souls make stands.

So let this tale of loss and love remind,

That in the chase for power, we may stray,

The dragon guards the pearl, but wisdom binds

The hearts that learn from darkness to find way.

For in the depths where shadows dare to tread,

True strength arises from the bonds we weave,

And in the light of love, where dreams are fed,

We find the pearl that we alone believe.

LIFE LESSONS

The tale of the Chinese Dragon and the Pearl is rich with symbolism and meaning, offering several valuable life lessons that resonate with both personal growth and cultural wisdom. In this story, the dragon represents power, authority, and the ability to harness natural forces, while the pearl symbolizes wisdom, prosperity, and the rewards of diligent effort. Together, they encapsulate themes that are integral to understanding life and success.

One key lesson from this myth is the importance of balance between power and wisdom. The dragon, despite its immense strength and authority, recognizes that true prosperity is not solely about power. Instead, it seeks the pearl, which signifies the knowledge and wisdom necessary to wield that power effectively.

This teaches us that possessing strength or authority is not enough; one must also cultivate wisdom to make informed decisions and foster positive outcomes. In our lives, this balance is essential—whether in leadership, relationships, or personal ambitions.

Another significant lesson is the idea of persistence and effort. The journey to obtain the pearl is not easy, requiring dedication and hard work. This aspect of the tale serves as a reminder that success often comes as a result of perseverance and a willingness to face challenges head-on. It encourages individuals to pursue their goals relentlessly, understanding that the rewards of hard work can lead to personal and communal prosperity. This lesson resonates across various domains, from career pursuits to personal projects, reinforcing the value of resilience.

The story also emphasizes the concept of connection to nature. The dragon, a creature deeply rooted in Chinese mythology, symbolizes humanity's relationship with the natural world. This connection is crucial in fostering respect for the environment and understanding our place within it. The pearl, emerging from the depths of the ocean, serves as a reminder of the treasures that nature can provide, urging us to protect and honor the natural world. This connection prompts us to consider sustainability and the impact of our actions on the environment.

Additionally, the tale highlights the theme of community and collaboration. The dragon's quest for the pearl is not a solitary endeavor; it involves interactions with other beings and the environment. This aspect of the story underscores the importance of collaboration and the idea that working together can lead to greater achievements. In our own lives, forming connections and supporting one another can lead to shared success and prosperity. It reinforces the notion that while individual effort is vital, community engagement enhances the journey toward goals.

The story of the Chinese Dragon and the Pearl offers profound life lessons about the balance of power and wisdom, the value of persistence, the connection to nature, and the importance of community. Engaging with these themes encourages individuals to cultivate both strength and knowledge, embrace hard work, respect the environment, and foster collaboration. This tale serves as a timeless reminder of the intertwined nature of power, wisdom, and the journey toward prosperity.

“The Jade Emperor and the Zodiac” – The Chinese legend of how the twelve animals of the zodiac were chosen, exploring destiny and personality.

This poem recounts the Chinese legend of the Jade Emperor, who organized a race to determine the twelve animals of the zodiac. Each animal represents different traits and characteristics, reflecting various aspects of human personality. The race, driven by ambition and cunning, reveals the interplay between strength, intelligence, and cooperation. The rat cleverly rides the ox to gain an advantage, while other animals showcase their unique qualities. Ultimately, the selection of the zodiac animals symbolizes the balance of fate and free will, emphasizing that true destiny is shaped by both individual efforts and the bonds formed within the community.

I

In ancient realms where whispered legends weave,

Beneath the vaulted dome of heaven's grace,

The Jade Emperor, sovereign of the skies,

Contemplated fate with a benevolent face.

His gaze swept o'er the valleys, rich and wide,

Where mountains crowned in mist kissed twilight's hue,

He sought to shape the year, to turn the tide,

And summon forth the beasts of every view.

With silken clouds like curtains drawn aside,

He gathered them beneath the moon's soft glow,

A symphony of hearts, each pulse a guide,

Destinies entwined in patterns yet unknown.

The rat, a spark of cunning in his eye,

The ox, a bastion of unwavering might,

The tiger, fierce, with dreams that dared to fly,

The rabbit danced in shadows, pure delight.

II

The Emperor proclaimed a race to claim

The order of the signs, a sacred call;

Each creature thrummed with hope, a fervent flame,

To earn a place where starry fates enthrall.

Anticipation rippled in the air,

As hearts prepared to carve their legacies;

The river shimmered, flowing strong and fair,

A mirror of their souls, their destinies.

Upon the day, the sky unfurled in gold,

A shimmering path where fortune's favor lay;

With thunderous roars, the race began to mold,

Each creature leaped, defying doubt's decay.

The rat, though small, with intellect ablaze,

Leaped upon the ox, a silent, shrewd decree;

In whispers spun of dreams, he found his ways,
The course of fate, a dance of bold esprit.
The tiger, king of shadows, quick and bright,
The dragon soared, a tempest on the wing,
While the horse ran wild, a spirit full of light,
And the sheep, with grace, in harmony would sing.
Each beast unveiled their essence, proud and free,
Yet deep within, a truth began to stir;
The dance of power, cooperation's plea,
For in the bonds of unity, they were.

III

As waters churned, the river swelled with pride,
The rat, with guile, beheld the distant shore;
He leaped ahead, while others fell aside,
Yet fate, a fickle mistress, craved much more.
As victory shone in the rat's keen eye,
The dragon, fierce, descended from the skies,
"I've soared for you, yet you remain awry,
For strength alone cannot the heavens rise."
In storm and fury, the dragon cast his spell,
A flash of scales igniting night's deep hue;
The creatures paused, caught in the magic's swell,

As destiny revealed its path anew.

The rooster's crow rang clear, a clarion call,

While the monkey swung, a jester in delight;

The dog, a guardian, stood strong and tall,

And the pig, content, basked in fortune's light.

Yet in the shadows, envy brewed and grew,

As serpents hissed with venom in their wake,

"A curse upon this race, this folly too!

Where greed prevails, the very ground will shake."

But the Emperor, with wisdom rich as time,

Stood firm, his presence grounding like the earth;

He knew that every heart held rhythm, rhyme,

Their fates were threads of love, a shared rebirth.

IV

As seasons turned, the signs adorned the sky,

The cycle spun, each year a tale retold;

The rat, the ox, the tiger, each did vie,

Their spirits woven into fabric bold.

The Jade Emperor, with knowing smile,

Looked down upon the realm where dreams take flight;

He grasped that destinies are forged in style,

Not solely by the race, but love's pure light.

So let this tale remind us of our thread,

In zodiac's embrace, where all align;

That fortune's dance is not a fleeting spread,

But in our hearts, where destinies entwine.

In every creature lies a story grand,

A thread of fate that weaves through time and space;

The jade is firm, yet soft beneath the hand,

And in each soul, a spark, a warm embrace.

LIFE LESSONS

The legend of the Jade Emperor and the Zodiac is a fascinating tale that imparts several meaningful life lessons related to destiny, personality, and the interconnectedness of all beings. In this story, the Jade Emperor, a powerful figure in Chinese mythology, organizes a race to determine which animals will represent the twelve signs of the zodiac. The lessons drawn from this legend resonate deeply with cultural values and personal growth.

One prominent lesson is the concept of destiny and fate. The race itself symbolizes the journey of life, where each animal represents different traits and characteristics. Some animals succeed due to their inherent qualities, while others face obstacles that reflect their personality. This teaches us that while we may have certain innate traits, our paths are influenced by choices and circumstances. Understanding this interplay between destiny and personal agency encourages individuals to recognize that they have the power to shape their futures, regardless of their starting point.

Another significant theme is the idea of self-awareness and embracing one's identity. Each zodiac animal embodies specific characteristics—like the cleverness of the Rat, the courage of the Tiger, or the diligence of the Ox. This emphasizes the importance of recognizing one's own strengths and weaknesses. By understanding our unique qualities, we can navigate life more effectively, making choices that align with our true selves. This lesson encourages self-reflection and acceptance, promoting personal growth and authenticity.

The story also highlights the value of perseverance and adaptability. Some animals face challenges during the race, yet they find ways to overcome obstacles. For instance, the clever Rat manages to ride on the back of the Ox to finish first. This illustrates the importance of adaptability in the face of difficulties. Life often presents unexpected challenges, and being resilient and resourceful can lead to success. This encourages individuals to embrace change and find innovative solutions to the problems they encounter.

Furthermore, the tale emphasizes the significance of community and collaboration. While each animal competes for a position in the zodiac, the race itself underscores the idea that all participants contribute to the overall narrative. This reflects the interconnectedness of life, where each individual plays a role in a larger community. The lesson here is about valuing relationships and supporting one another, understanding that our lives are enriched by collaboration and shared experiences.

The legend of the Jade Emperor and the Zodiac imparts valuable life lessons about destiny, self-awareness, perseverance, and community. Engaging with these themes encourages individuals to embrace their unique identities, recognize their agency in shaping their destinies, adapt to challenges, and value the connections they share with others. This story serves as a timeless reminder of the complexities of life and the importance of understanding both ourselves and the world around us.

"The Legend of El Dorado" – The myth of a golden city hidden in South America, symbolizing greed and exploration.

The poem "The Legend of El Dorado" explores the mythical quest for a fabled city of gold in South America, symbolizing humanity's insatiable greed and desire for wealth. It follows the journey of conquistadors driven by ambition and longing, who traverse treacherous jungles and mountains in search of the elusive El Dorado. As they confront nature's fierce beauty and their own inner demons, they learn that the true treasure lies not in gold, but in wisdom and truth. Ultimately, the poem reflects on the futility of greed and the deeper riches found in love, connection, and the present moment.

I

In shadows cast by emerald leaves, where whispers dwell,

A tale unfolds, of gilded dreams and hearts that swell.

Through valleys deep, where serpents coil 'round rivers bright,

The quest for El Dorado sings—a siren's light.

A realm of promise veiled in mists of ancient lore,

Where sunlit spires rise, aglow on forgotten shore.

The fevered search ignites the soul, ambition's fire,

Each heart a vessel, yearning vast, a fierce desire.

Conquistadors with gleaming swords, their visions grand,

Through jungles thick, they tread the path, with fate unplanned.

Maps etched with hope in trembling hands chart the night,
Each glint upon the stream a fleeting, fateful light.
Yet nature's breath, wild, fierce, and untamed, stirs their dread,
The cries of jaguars echo deep, where shadows spread.
In rustling leaves, old tales of truth and sorrow spin,
Yet man, relentless, presses on, blind to the din.
Oh, El Dorado, phantom land, your lure is strong,
To chase a city forged in dreams, where souls belong.
Each heart a chalice filled with greed, yet yearning too,
For something more than gold can give—a vision true.

II

Into the thicket bold they tread, through trials grim,
Where shadows dance, and daylight wanes, their hopes grow dim.
The echoes of a thousand souls, lost in pursuit,
Laughter fades, replaced by cries—a mournful flute.
They seek the king, adorned in gold, a spectral guise,
With offerings of wealth and wit, they pierce the skies.
Through mountains high, they toil and strain, ambition's plight,
While dreams of glory shimmer bright, then vanish from sight.
In haunted glades beneath the stars, they pause to rest,
Yet visions of the golden dawn invade their weary quest.
Each glimmer from the distant peaks, a phantom flame,

With every turn, a tale of woe, a whispered name.

The rivers churn with secrets deep of those who've strayed,

A lineage of wanderers, in shadows weighed.

The air is thick with tales of greed, of trust betrayed,

As comets blaze across the night, their fates displayed.

Yet still they march, through night's embrace, their spirits fierce,

Each footfall echoes legends lost, each heart to pierce.

The city's glow, a beacon far, though shadows grow,

Their dreams entwined with every leaf, as rivers flow.

III

At last they stand upon the vale, a vision grand,

Where golden walls rise from the earth, as if by hand.

A cacophony of joy erupts; they fall to knees,

For in this light, their hopes ignite, like whispered pleas.

But lo! The guardian, fierce and wise, with gaze aflame,

Stands sentinel 'gainst dreams of greed, to thwart their claim.

With words of ancient wisdom flows, a warning clear,

"Your hearts are heavy with desire; relinquish fear."

For El Dorado's heart is not of gold, but truth,

A radiant spark of dreams fulfilled—the wisdom of youth.

Yet greed, like ivy, creeps and binds, consumes the mind,

As men, entranced by shining dreams, leave reason blind.

The earth beneath them trembles soft, the skies grow dim,

As shadows of their avarice rise—a haunting hymn.

With trembling hands, they reach for gold, for fleeting gleam,

But find it turns to dust, as dreams dissolve in dream.

In frantic rush, they fight and claw, consumed by need,

Yet all they touch turns cold and bare, their hearts concede.

For in the quest, they've lost the path, their souls laid bare,

El Dorado's truth is lost to those who dare.

IV

Now as the dawn breaks through the mist, a quiet grace,

The legend lingers, woven deep in time and space.

For every quest for golden realms holds shadows tight,

Yet truth resides in hearts that seek beyond the light.

The myth of El Dorado shines, a mirror held,

Reflecting greed and dreams entwined, where wisdom swelled.

In every tale of treasure sought, a lesson blooms,

That gold may glitter bright, but wisdom's voice consumes.

So wanderers, take heed of tales where shadows play,

For in the search for golden realms, we often stray.

El Dorado is not a place, but in the heart,

A city built of love and truth, where dreams impart.

And when the sun sets on your quest, let go the chase,

Embrace the beauty of the now, the quiet grace.

For gold is fleeting, but the soul's true wealth abides,

In stories shared and love embraced, where hope resides.

LIFE LESSONS

The legend of El Dorado, the fabled city of gold, encapsulates several profound life lessons about greed, the quest for knowledge, and the human spirit's resilience. This myth, rooted in the stories of explorers and indigenous cultures, offers insights that resonate across time and cultures.

One of the most prominent lessons from the tale is the danger of greed. The allure of El Dorado draws countless adventurers and explorers, leading them to pursue wealth at any cost. This relentless quest often results in destructive consequences, including environmental degradation, violence, and the exploitation of indigenous peoples. The story serves as a cautionary tale, reminding us that an insatiable desire for material wealth can blind individuals to the values of humanity, compassion, and ethical responsibility. It emphasizes the importance of recognizing when ambition crosses the line into greed, urging us to consider the impact of our desires on ourselves and others.

Another critical lesson is the significance of exploration and discovery. While the pursuit of El Dorado is often portrayed as misguided, the underlying theme of exploration highlights the human desire to seek knowledge and understanding. The explorers' journeys reflect a fundamental aspect of human nature—the quest for new experiences and insights. This serves as a reminder that exploration, both literal and metaphorical, can lead to personal growth and enlightenment. However, it is essential to approach such quests with humility and respect for the cultures and environments encountered along the way.

The legend also emphasizes the importance of resilience and adaptability. Many who sought El Dorado faced immense challenges, including treacherous landscapes, harsh climates, and internal conflicts. Their experiences teach us that perseverance in the face of adversity is crucial. The ability to adapt to changing circumstances and learn from failures can lead to growth and success in unexpected ways. This lesson resonates in our own lives, encouraging us to embrace challenges as opportunities for development rather than as insurmountable obstacles.

Furthermore, the myth underscores the concept of illusion versus reality. The idea of El Dorado represents a utopia, a place of unimaginable wealth and happiness. However, the reality often falls short of such ideals, revealing the complexity of human desires. This lesson reminds us to critically evaluate our aspirations and recognize that true fulfillment often lies not in material riches but in meaningful relationships, experiences, and personal integrity.

The legend of El Dorado provides valuable insights into the complexities of human ambition and desire. It cautions against the pitfalls of greed, celebrates the spirit of exploration, underscores the importance of resilience, and invites reflection on the nature of reality versus illusion. Engaging with these themes encourages individuals to pursue their dreams with integrity, seek knowledge responsibly, and embrace the journey of life with an open heart and mind.

"The Tale of the Baba Yaga" – A Russian folktale about a witch who lives in a house that walks on chicken legs, symbolizing fear and the unknown.

"The Tale of Baba Yaga" is a retelling of a classic Russian folktale featuring the witch Baba Yaga, who lives in a magical hut that stands on chicken legs. The poem follows Vasilisa, a brave maiden seeking wisdom and light to dispel the darkness in her life. To earn Baba Yaga's favor, Vasilisa must complete three daunting tasks: gathering fire from restless spirits, retrieving water from a well of sorrow, and fetching a feather from a crow. Through her journey, she confronts her fears and emerges transformed, discovering that wisdom often lies hidden within the shadows of the unknown.

I

In the heart of the forest, where shadows weave and twine,

Amongst the whispering birches, dark tales begin to shine.

There stands a hut, a creature's lair, upon its chicken legs,

A sentinel of secrets deep, where night's enchantment begs.

Baba Yaga, witch of fate, with hair spun silver-white,

Her eyes, twin pools of midnight, cradle dreams wrapped tight.

She brews her potions thick as fog in cauldrons blackened deep,

And every spell she casts awakens ancient sleep.

The air is thick with murmurs of long-forgotten lore,

Of lost souls who dared to wander past the forest door.

Children huddle close, while mothers tell their tales of fright,

Of the witch who roams the woods, a specter cloaked in night.

A crone with powers vast, yet heart ensnared by pain,

In solitude she weaves the threads of joy and bitter bane.

Legends twist around her, like ivy 'round the trees,

Her laughter echoes hauntingly, entwined in midnight's breeze.

In twilight's tender glow, as shadows start to blend,

The bravest venture forth, with fate as their only friend.

To seek the truth of Baba Yaga, both feared and revered,

In her realm of magic, where destinies are seared.

II

One fateful eve, a maiden bold, with courage fierce and bright,

Ventured deep into the woods, beneath the cloak of night.

Her name was Vasilisa, a heart of purest gold,

A thread of fate entwined her path, a story yet untold.

With lantern's flicker casting light on gnarled roots and stones,

She wandered through the silence, where the wildness moans.

The forest whispered warnings, yet she pressed on ahead,

For in her heart, a quest was born, to face her deepest dread.

She sought a gift from Baba Yaga, a spark to light her way,

To banish darkness from her life, to turn the night to day.

But tales of fear encircled her, like shadows closing in,
Would she emerge as victor, or succumb to primal sin?
The moonlight danced upon her skin, a cloak of silver light,
With every step, the ancient trees murmured tales of night.
Yet Vasilisa, undaunted, felt a fire in her soul,
A whisper from her ancestors, urging her toward her goal.
At last, the hut appeared, a sight both strange and grand,
It twisted in the twilight, like a beast that would withstand.
With heart a-thunder, she approached, her breath a fragile thread,
And there, within the doorway, stood the witch of dread.

III

"Enter, child," the crone intoned, her voice like crackling flame,
"Do you seek to know my secrets, to unlock your heart's true name?"
With trembling hands, Vasilisa stepped across the threshold wide,
And felt the weight of ages past, the stories deep inside.
"Speak, and I shall listen," Baba Yaga's gaze was keen,
"Yet know the price of knowledge, and the darkness that's unseen."
The room was filled with shadows, alive with whispered lies,
Each corner held a memory, each crevice held their sighs.
"Bring me a task," the maiden cried, her voice a steady flame,
"To prove my worth, to stand with pride, to carve out my own name."
The witch, with eyes that pierced the night, a smile creased her lips,

"Three tasks I shall set for you; embrace the night's eclipse."

The first, to gather fire from the hearts of wailing ghosts,

To coax their flames and draw them forth, amidst their haunting boasts.

With fear but also courage, Vasilisa took her leave,

Through thorns and shadows, she would weave what few could dare believe.

The second, find the waters from the well of lost despair,

Where tears of sorrow mingle, in a realm stripped bare.

The third, to fetch a feather from the crow's unyielding heart,

A symbol of resilience, to bind her tale apart.

In darkness thick and twisted paths, she ventured forth anew,

Each step a dance with destiny, each breath a song so true.

The echoes of the forest sang of trials yet to come,

Yet Vasilisa pressed onward, with the beating of her drum.

IV

At dawn, she returned, her heart ablaze, her spirit bright,

With fire forged from wailing souls and waters pure as light.

The feather clasped within her hands, a gift from shadow's flight,

Baba Yaga, nodding wise, beheld her with delight.

"You've faced the fears that haunt the night and conquered what was dark,

In every task, you found the truth, ignited passion's spark.

Now learn, dear child, the witch's heart holds power fierce and wild,

But fear not what you cannot see; embrace the unbeguiled."

For Baba Yaga is not merely fear, nor darkness' heavy shroud,

But wisdom woven in the night, in laughter rich and loud.

With every tale that curls like smoke upon the forest floor,

The unknown beckons with a voice, revealing ancient lore.

And so Vasilisa emerged, not just with gifts in hand,

But wisdom steeped in shadows deep, a strength to understand.

For in the dance of fear and hope, the wild and the divine,

Resides the magic of the heart, in tales of old entwined.

As dawn embraced the waking world, the witch became a guide,

A bridge between the known and not, where truths and dreams collide.

In her hut, on chicken legs, a tale forever spun,

Of courage found in darkness deep, where fear and love are one.

LIFE LESSONS

The Tale of Baba Yaga is a rich Russian folktale that imparts several important life lessons through its exploration of fear, the unknown, and the complexities of human nature. Baba Yaga, often portrayed as a fearsome witch with ambiguous motives, embodies both danger and wisdom, offering insights into navigating life's challenges.

One of the key lessons from the story is the importance of confronting fear. Baba Yaga represents the fears that often loom in our lives—the unknown, the powerful, and the unpredictable. Characters in the tale who encounter her must confront their fears head-on, which teaches us that avoidance can lead to greater anxiety. By facing what we fear, we often discover that these fears are not as daunting as they seem. This lesson encourages resilience and bravery, reminding us that growth often comes from stepping outside our comfort zones.

The story also emphasizes the significance of understanding and respect for nature. Baba Yaga lives in a house that stands on chicken legs, which can move and dance, symbolizing the wild and unpredictable aspects of the natural world. This illustrates the idea that nature is powerful and should be respected. In our modern lives, this lesson remains relevant, reminding us to honor the environment and recognize our connection to the natural world. It encourages stewardship and a deeper appreciation for the complexities of life beyond human control.

Additionally, the tale underscores the theme of wisdom in unexpected places. Baba Yaga is often depicted as a source of knowledge and guidance, despite her fearsome demeanor. Characters who approach her with humility and respect can gain valuable insights. This teaches us that wisdom can come from unexpected sources and that we should remain open to learning from everyone, regardless of their appearance or reputation. It prompts us to seek knowledge actively and to listen to those who may have experienced more of life's challenges.

Moreover, the tale highlights the notion of duality in human nature. Baba Yaga embodies both nurturing and destructive qualities, reflecting the complexities of human behavior. This duality reminds us that people cannot be easily categorized as good or evil; rather, we all possess a mix of traits that can manifest in various ways. Understanding this complexity fosters empathy, helping us to navigate relationships and recognize that everyone has their struggles.

In conclusion, The Tale of Baba Yaga imparts valuable lessons about confronting fear, respecting nature, seeking wisdom from unexpected sources, and understanding the duality of human nature. Engaging with these themes encourages personal growth, resilience, and a deeper appreciation for the complexities of life and relationships. Through Baba Yaga's story, we are reminded that the journey through fear and the unknown can lead to profound insights and personal transformation.

Epilogue

As we close the pages of "Legends and Lessons: 36 Myths Unveiled", we find ourselves standing at the intersection of ancient wisdom and modern life. These myths, rich with the essence of human experience, serve as mirrors reflecting our own journeys—our struggles, hopes, and the timeless quest for understanding. Each poem and its accompanying lessons invite us to explore the depths of our emotions and the breadth of our aspirations.

In the echoes of Prometheus's defiance, we are reminded of the power of rebellion and the price of knowledge. Orpheus's tragic tale teaches us about love's enduring strength and the pain of loss. The cunning of Anansi encourages us to embrace cleverness, while the bravery of Beowulf inspires us to confront our fears head-on.

These stories transcend time, reminding us that the human spirit is resilient and capable of profound transformation. Just as the phoenix rises from its ashes, we too can find renewal amidst life's challenges. The lessons embedded within these narratives are not merely historical artifacts; they are guides to navigating our contemporary world.

As you reflect on these myths, consider how they resonate with your own life. Each legend is a thread in the rich tapestry of existence, weaving together themes of fate, bravery, love, and wisdom. Embrace these lessons, let them guide you in moments of doubt, and inspire you in times of triumph.

Thank you for embarking on this journey through the realms of myth and poetry. May the stories continue to illuminate your path, fostering a deeper connection to the lessons of the past as you forge your own future. Remember, the wisdom of the ancients is ever-present, waiting to inspire and guide those who seek it.

About Alex Telman

Alex Telman is a renowned Spiritual Healer based in Brisbane, Australia. He is celebrated for his profound influence on the mind and spirit, he was a pioneering leader in the self-help movement of the 1980s. Alex has dedicated over 45 years to empowering individuals to transform their lives through healing and inspiration.

From an early age, Alex's fascination with the Spirit guided him toward a path of deep insight, where he skillfully blends traditional spiritual practices with contemporary therapeutic techniques. His impressive academic credentials include degrees in Law, Arts, Hypnotherapy, and Education, providing him with a comprehensive understanding of psychic phenomena and the spiritual dimensions of everyday life. His diverse clientele ranges from natural health practitioners and spiritual healers to celebrities and business leaders, all seeking his unique wisdom and guidance.

Beyond his healing practice, Alex is a prolific poet whose works encompass sonnets, sestinas, and modern poetic forms. His poetry captures the essence of life in both urban and rural settings, delving into the psychological and philosophical depths of the human experience. Recognized for their profound insight, his poems weave realism with emotional richness, offering readers a deeper understanding of life's complexities.

As an esteemed author and dynamic public speaker, Alex masterfully combines his expertise in the fields of spiritual healing, transformative psychology and poetry, to inspire others toward greater clarity and self-awareness. His commitment to community engagement fosters personal and collective transformation, ensuring that each client receives the care and attention they deserve. Alex Telman's journey is a testament to the transformative power of healing and self-expression, illuminating pathways to richer, more meaningful lives.

In Brisbane's heart, where city lights embrace,

A spirit thrives where timeless truths entwine—

Alex Telman, whose quest for light and grace

Unites the ancient wisdom with the modern line.

Since youth, the Spirit's call was pure and bright,

A journey through the mists of deepened lore;

In realms of arcane art and healing's light,

He navigates where hidden truths implore.

His sonnets chart the human heart's vast sweep,

Where light and dark in delicate balance play—

Each line a beacon in the night's deep sleep,

Unveiling depths where inner truths hold sway.

A healer's gift, a poet's rare finesse,

In Alex's work, both mind and soul find rest.

Don't miss out!

Visit the website below and you can sign up to receive emails whenever Alex Telman publishes a new book. There's no charge and no obligation.

https://books2read.com/r/B-A-YBSCC-QHDEF

BOOKS 2 READ

Connecting independent readers to independent writers.

www.ingramcontent.com/pod-product-compliance
Lightning Source LLC
LaVergne TN
LVHW010055170826
845678LV00012B/2142

* 9 7 9 8 2 3 0 9 3 5 5 4 4 *